The Study of the
Synoptic Gospels

New approaches and outlooks

The Study of the Synoptic Gospels

New approaches and outlooks

Augustin Cardinal Bea, S.J.

English version edited by
Joseph A. Fitzmyer, S.J.

HARPER & ROW, PUBLISHERS

New York.

LIBRARY OF CONGRESS CATALOG CARD NUMBER: 65-20447

Contents

EDITOR'S PREFACE   7

FOREWORD   9

I

THE HISTORICITY OF THE SYNOPTIC GOSPELS FROM A
HUMAN POINT OF VIEW   13
1. The methodology of Form Criticism   17
2. The reasons for such a position   20
3. Presuppositions or theoretical postulates of Form
   Criticism   21
4. Methods and procedures of Form Criticism   27
5. Form in which the Gospel message was originally
   presented and transmitted   33
6. The function of the evangelists   40
7. Conclusion   43

II

THE HISTORICAL CHARACTER OF THE SYNOPTIC GOSPELS
CONSIDERED AS INSPIRED WRITINGS   45
1. The inspiration of the sacred books and its
   consequences for the inspired authors' manner of
   writing   48
2. Psychological reflections on the manner of
   narrating and presenting an event   51

3. Attitudes towards the differences among the
   Gospels   60
4. The tasks of different groups in the Church
   engaged in the interpretation of the Gospels   70
5. Conclusion   75

APPENDIX: Instruction concerning the Historical Truth
of the Gospels   79

LIST OF ABBREVIATIONS   91

INDEX   93

Editor's Preface

In the Foreword Cardinal Bea explains the origin of the little book which is here being presented to the English-speaking world. An English version of it was circulated among the Council Fathers at the first session of the Second Vatican Council (1962). A considerably modified Italian version of it, issued as a commentary on the Instruction of the Biblical Commission, was later published in the *Civiltà cattolica* in two instalments: "La storicità dei Vangeli sinottici" (6 June 1964, pp. 417–36), and "Il carattere storico dei Vangeli sinottici come opere ispirate" (20 June 1964, pp. 526–45). Subsequently, the two articles, together with slight changes and with the text of the Biblical Commission's Instruction, were published in the form of a booklet entitled, *La storicità dei Vangeli* (Brescia, Morcelliana, 1964). My task has merely been to see that the English version prepared in 1962 conforms with that of the Morcelliana Italian edition which represents the Cardinal's most recent presentation of this subject.

Many commentaries will undoubtedly appear on the Biblical Commission's Instruction.[1] But all who are

---

[1] The interested reader will find further commentaries on the Instruction in the following articles:

J. DELORME, "La vérité historique des évangiles: Instruction de la Commission Pontificale pour les Études Bibliques", *L'ami du clergé* **74** (17 September 1964), 554–9. E. GALBIATI, "L'istruzione della Commissione Biblica sul valore storico dei Vangeli", *Scuola cattolica* **92** (1964), 303–10. C. KEARNS, "The Instruction on the Historical Truth of the Gospels: Some First Impressions", *Angelicum* **41** (1964), 218–34. N. LOHFINK, "Die Evangelien und die Geschichte: Zur Instruktion vom 21 April 1964", *Stimmen der Zeit* **174** (August 1964), 365–74.

acquainted with Cardinal Bea's position as a former rector of the Pontifical Biblical Institute in Rome and as a member of the Biblical Commission itself will readily appreciate the value of having from his pen this sensitive treatment of a delicate and important subject.

JOSEPH A. FITZMYER, S.J.

J. RADERMAKERS, "Instruction du 21 avril 1964 sur la vérité historique des évangiles", *La nouvelle revue théologique* 96 (1964), 634–43.

The Editor's own commentary, "The Biblical Commission's Instruction on the Historical Truth of the Gospels", appeared in *Theological Studies* 25 (1964), 286–408, and has been reprinted as a Paulist Press Pamphlet entitled, *The Historical Truth of the Gospels: The 1964 Instruction of Biblical Commission* (Glen Rock, N.J., 1965).

Foreword

To a biblical scholar this booklet may appear very elementary, if not banal. But it is not written for biblical scholars. During the first session of the Second Vatican Council a number of my brother bishops asked me—and very insistently—to compose for them a brief, clear, and easily understandable exposé of the questions raised by Form Criticism. This matter had been causing them concern and anxiety, since it often seemed that proponents of this mode of criticism had been undermining the historical value of the Gospels. In answer to this request, I composed a text which was mimeographed and destined for a private and restricted circulation. But when the Instruction of the Pontifical Biblical Commission appeared,[1] dealing with the historicity of the Gospels, a number of friends thought that what I had written for the bishops might serve as a commentary on the Instruction and prove useful for priests and laymen whose occupations precluded a study of books of greater length, depth, and detail. It is to meet the needs of such readers—and not to offer a contribution to technical biblical scholarship—that I give this brief sketch to the public.

The recent Instruction of the Biblical Commission, to be found in the Appendix, is at once dense, concise, and positive. It is obviously concerned to encourage biblical

[1] "Instructio de historica Evangeliorum veritate", *L'osservatore romano*, 14 May 1964, p. 3. The Instruction was approved by Pope Paul VI and dated 21 April 1964. The official text of it is found in *AAS* 56 (1964), 712–18.

scholarship and to protect biblical scholars from the impatience sometimes manifested towards them. It gives its approval to the most modern and scientific methods of biblical research; it indicates the complexity of many problems of Gospel exegesis; and, while warning against the intrusion of dubious philosophical and theological presuppositions into exegetical matters, it approves of the methodology of a sane and balanced Form Criticism. It takes pains to indicate the three stages in which the Gospel message has come down to us: from Christ's own words and actions to the apostles, and from them to the writers of the Gospels. The Instruction ends by recalling that ultimately the purpose of biblical studies is pastoral, that is, concerned with man's salvation. Though this is not the immediate end of every specific investigation, nevertheless it should never be wholly forgotten.

This booklet will certainly come into the hands of readers not particularly acquainted with its mode of treating the Gospels. More than one of them will wonder about the import of such a document from the Biblical Commission. The Pontifical Biblical Commission was established more than fifty years ago to help Roman Catholics find an orientation in difficult biblical questions. Its members are cardinals, and today they number fifteen, belonging to ten different nationalities. They are aided by thirty-two consultors or experts, drawn from eleven different countries. The spirit of the Biblical Commission in the early days of its existence was expressed in the very title of the papal document which set it up, *Vigilantiae* (Apostolic Letter of Pope Leo XIII in 1902). Many of the responses it issued in the early part of this century were negative and restrictive. But in more recent times it has become a positive force in the Catholic Church, implementing the directives of Pope Pius XII in his *magna charta* of biblical studies, *Divino afflante Spiritu* (encyclical of 1943). The issuing of the recent Instruction on the Historical Truth of the Gospels is unprecedented in its positive and forward-looking approach to the Gospels. Except for the cautions it expresses about philosophical presuppositions and the excesses of preachers and popularizers, its tone is calm, suggestive, and illuminating. Even those who do not feel any obligation to heed the Instruction of the Biblical Commission, such as our Separated Brethren, will not fail to mark the difference in this Instruction and the support that it is giving to the modern study of the Gospels. It is legitimate to think that our treatment of this important question, which is a source of no little concern to many even outside the Roman Catholic communion, will make the Instruction and its import a little more intelligible to them.

As a commentary on the recent Instruction, this book aims at explaining the profound reasons for what is stated and proposed in it. It seeks to show above all how the results of the most modern research and studies on the Gospels are consonant with the age-old principles of Catholic exegesis. Not only may these results be utilized by the Catholic commentator who would live up to the tradition of his forebears in explaining the word of God to the faithful, but he must use them. The fact that not a few of these results have been achieved by the labours of New Testament scholars outside the Roman Catholic Church is lost on no one. But the support that is given in the recent Instruction of the Biblical Commission to the type of interpretation which uses these results is noteworthy and should not lightly be passed over. It is to be hoped then that this book will also be of interest to our brothers who do not belong to the Roman Catholic Church—especially now when Christian confessions are mutually seeking to know each other better.

I

The historicity of the Synoptic Gospels from a human point of view

Everyone who is acquainted with the present status of Catholic exegesis, and in particular with that of the Gospels, will recognize the great importance of the recent Instruction of the Pontifical Biblical Commission on the Historical Truth of the Gospels. For there was, and still is, a whole series of important questions about them which can best be summed up under the heading, "the application of the principles of the encyclical of Pope Pius XII, *Divino afflante Spiritu*, to the interpretation of the Gospels". This immediately implies—again after two decades of meditation and study on that encyclical—a fresh consideration of this fundamental document. For its importance and modernity are constantly being revealed to us.

The proximate occasion of the publication of the recent Instruction is the fact that today there is a proliferation of writings which question the truth of the sayings and events contained in the Gospels. The Instruction speaks of this situation in general and does not state that this is happening specifically among Catholics. But the result of it is to create notable bewilderment and perplexity not only in the circle of the specialists, but more widely in the whole Catholic world. Consequently, the need has been felt for some time now of an official document that would clarify the situation.[1]

To understand the nature of the basic problem discussed in the Instruction, some reference must be made to Form Criticism which in the last half century has posed the problem of the historicity of the Gospels in a new and special way. In an effort to explain the genesis of the Gospels, the proponents of this method of criticism have often affirmed that the setting in which the Gospel message originally took shape was the primitive Christian community which resembles the popular setting where legends are born. Such settings are indeed both creative and susceptible to influence from ambient cultures. These two factors give rise to alterations and deformations of the primitive content. Now it is said that the Gospel message, before being fixed in writing, was exposed in this way to alterations, intrusions, and in part at least to serious deformations. Given such a point of view, a problem naturally arises for the Catholic exegete: what is the credibility and the historical value of the Gospels accounts? Do they really give us an authentic picture of the life and the teaching of Jesus?

Now this generic problem can be posed in a twofold way —or in two stages. One can ask, first of all in general, whether the Gospels are documents of historical value, whether they really intend to report faithfully events which

[1] Our commentary on the Instruction will not follow it literally step by step. It begins rather with the heart of the problem itself and tries to treat it in a systematic way. Reference will be made from time to time to the pertinent passages of the Instruction. In this way the density of the teaching set forth in the Instruction will be apparent, as well as the import of the principles proposed.

historically occurred, and whether they actually do so in a
way that makes their testimony trustworthy. Secondly, the
problem can be posed by beginning with the presupposition
of Catholic teaching that the Gospels are inspired by God.
They enjoy an absolute inerrancy because their primary and
principal author is God who is truth itself, whereas every
work of man, even of the best informed and best motivated,
is always subject to the danger of error. If this is so, the
question arises: how is one to judge the differences in the
various Gospels as they recount the same event or report the
same saying of Jesus? For it is well known that even the
most crucial words of the Lord, such as the Our Father and
the words with which he instituted the Eucharist, are not
recorded by the Gospels in a fully uniform manner, but
rather with variations. Hence the question: how does one
explain these facts and show that the Gospels actually do
state what historically occurred and that there is no error in
the way in which they state it, but rather that this is perfectly
consonant historical truth?

These two ways of considering the Gospels and their
historicity find counterparts in the Instruction of the Biblical
Commission itself. For it states that one must apply to the
Gospels, as to any other human composition, the criteria of
the historical method (par. IV).[1] At the same time, one must
keep in mind that the apostles in their preaching were filled
with the Holy Spirit and were guided by him; and further-
more that the Gospels were written under the inspiration of
the Holy Spirit who guarded the authors from all error

---

[1] References to the Instruction will be given in this way. The Roman numerals
correspond to those used in the translation of the Instruction found in the appendix,
pp. 79–89. *Editor.*

(par. XI). In this first chapter, then, we begin by treating only the first of these two aspects of the problem. The second— that concerned with inspiration and inerrancy—will form the subject of Chapter II.[1]

The first step, then, is to explain and evaluate the essential points of Form Criticism, that is, its main theoretical pre- suppositions and its methodology. When this has been done, it will be possible to propose an explanation of the salient data and the main problems arising from this method and to draw the proper conclusions bearing on the historicity of the Synoptic Gospels. Our aim is to show that the Gospels, even aside from their divine inspiration and considered solely from a purely human and historical point of view, are worthy of credence; that their testimony fully merits con- sideration. Since Form Criticism has cast doubt not only on the Catholic doctrine of the divine inspiration of the Gospels, but also on their purely human historical value, there is need to establish, first of all, this very value. It is an essential factor, and constitutes the indispensable foundation for all the rest. As Pope Leo XIII remarked, "Since the divine and infallible magisterium of the Church rests also on the authority of Holy Scripture, the first thing to be done is to vindicate the trustworthiness of the sacred records, at least as human documents.'[2]

---

[1] To be more precise, we note now that we shall be dealing with the Synoptic Gospels only, since the method of Form Criticism which posed the problem under discussion pertains above all to these Gospels. The problem of the historical value of the Johannine Gospel can also be raised and has been raised—but for other reasons which do not concern us here.

[2] *Providentissimus Deus* (EB 116; ASS 26[1893–4]284; RSS 19): "huius[Scripturae] propterea fides saltem humana asserenda vindicandaque est."

1. The methodology of Form Criticism

Form Criticism aims at explaining the origin of our Gospels, by reconstructing the "history", that is, the genesis and the development, of the "forms" in which the Gospel message was presented, preached, and passed on, until it was definitely fixed in the Gospels as we have them today.[1] More precisely, it is a question of the "history of the *formation*" of the Gospels.

To understand Form Criticism, we must take into account the various sources on which it has drawn, especially literary criticism, sociology, and the history of religions. The early proponents of Form Criticism, in interpreting the New Testament and especially the Gospels, were inspired princi-

---

[1] We give here a brief introductory bibliography. Most of the works are by Catholic authors. For the sake of convenience recent works especially have been cited. The citation of an article or book obviously does not signify approval of everything contained therein.

A. *On Form Criticism:*

P. BENOIT, "Réflexions sur la 'Formgeschichtliche Methode' ", *Revue biblique* 53 (1946), 481–512 (ample bibliography).

A. DESCAMPS, "Perspectives actuelles dans l'exégèse des Synoptiques", *Revue diocésaine de Tournai* 8 (1953), 3–16, 401–14, 497–523.

C. H. DODD, *The Parables of the Kingdom* (London, 1953).

E. FLORIT, *Il metodo della "Storia delle forme" e sua applicazione al racconto della Passione* (Roma, 1935).

X. LÉON-DUFOUR, "Aux sources des évangiles", *Introduction à la Bible* 2 (Paris, 1959), 297–305; "Formgeschichte et Redaktionsgeschichte des Évangiles synoptiques", *Recherches de science religieuse* 46 (1958), 237–69.

L. J. McGINLEY, *Form Criticism of the Synoptic Healing Narratives* (Woodstock, 1944).

H. RIESENFELD, *The Gospel Tradition and Its Beginnings* (London, 1957).

E. SCHICK, *Formgeschichte und Synoptikerexegese* (Münster, 1940).

J. M. ROBINSON, *Kerygma und historischer Jesus* (Zürich, 1960) [a new edition of *A New Quest of the Historical Jesus* (London-Naperville, 1959)].

V. TAYLOR, *The Formation of the Gospel Tradition* (London, 1933).

J. HEUSCHEN, ed., *La formation des évangiles: Problème synoptique et Formgeschichte. Recherches Bibliques II* (Bruges-Paris, 1957).

pally by the work of H. Gunkel on literary forms and on the formation of the books of Genesis and the Psalms.[1] The studies of Gunkel and of other Old Testament scholars who furthered his work served as a model for the Form Critics. In applying to the Gospel narratives the findings of all these studies and disciplines, Form Criticism seeks to understand the genesis of the present text of the Synoptic Gospels. Through literary criticism of the present Gospels, it uncovers the smallest units which existed prior to the present Gospel framework and determines the "literary forms" of these smaller elements (for example, "sayings and maxims", "controversies", "miracle stories", etc.). It also seeks to fix the *Sitz im Leben* (or *vital context*) of these smaller elements.

Now this *Sitz im Leben*, the cradle in which the Gospel message was born and grew, is said to have been *the primitive Christian community*. To understand the work of this community with respect to the Gospels, one must first of all

B. *On the Historicity of the Gospels*

   C. H. DODD, *History and the Gospels* (London, 1938).

   J. GUITTON, *Jésus* (Paris, 1956).

   X. LÉON-DUFOUR, in J. Huby, *L'évangile et les évangiles* (nouv. éd. revue et augmentée; Paris, 1954), pp. 41–74; in *Bulletin du Comité des Études de St Sulpice* **35** (1961), 342–64 (ample bibliography); *Les évangiles et l'histoire de Jésus* (Paris, 1963).

   F. MUSSNER, "Der historische Jesus und der Christus des Glaubens", *Biblische Zeitschrift* (1957), 224–52.

   B. RIGAUX, "L'historicité de Jésus devant l'exégèse récente", *Revue biblique* **65** (1958), 481–522.

   H. RISTOW and K. MATHIAE, *Der historische Jesus und der kerygmatische Christus*, (Berlin, 1960). Especially recommended is the section by H. Schürmann, "Die vorösterlichen Anfänge der Logien-Tradition. Ein Versuch eines formgeschichtlichen Zugangs zum Leben Jesu", pp. 342–70.

   R. SCHNACKENBURG, "Jesusforschung und Christusglaube", *Catholica* **13** (1959), 1–17.

   V. TAYLOR, *The Life and Ministry of Jesus* (London, 1954).

[1] *Genesis* (Handkommentar zum A. T.; Göttingen, 1901; 5th ed., 1922). *Einleitung in die Psalmen* (Göttingen, 1933).

understand the community itself. According to the Form Critics, analysis of the New Testament and especially of the Gospels shows that the primitive community from which the Gospels come to us (or better, from which what the Gospels narrate come to us) was quite similar to popular milieux, or anonymous masses, in which legends are born. According to at least one group of Form Critics the primitive community neither had nor was able to have an interest in history since it lived in eager expectation of the imminent end of the world and of the glorious coming of Christ. What would be the point of such a community being interested in history, that is, in past events? Even apart from this view of the eschatological school the question arises: what possible interest in history could be had by common men such as the apostles and the simple folk of the primitive community?

The Form Critics speak of "legends", because the Gospels are a product of "faith", and not of history. Faith and the attitude of an historian are incompatible; faith is nothing more than the taking of a stand in favour of the object, whereas the attitude of an historian must of necessity be absolutely objective and impartial. As the principle phrased by Tacitus has it, the historian must write *sine ira et studio* (without passion and attachment).[1]

Another characteristic of the community, of the popular environment in which the Gospel was born and grew, was that it was "creative". Impressed by some act or word recounted by those who saw it or heard it, the community further developed it—explaining, drawing on its imagination to make additions, borrowing from the religious ideas of its environment to clarify and increase the original data.

[1] *Annales*, I.I.

Thus the original material grew in size and was handed down in ever increasing quantities.

2. *The reasons for such a position*

And the proof? The reply to this question is that literary criticism permits one to pass through diverse strata, as it were, and in the process isolate first the larger groupings of passages and then the small, primary units. These are labelled, according to the literary forms variously assigned by different critics, as "sayings and maxims", "miracle stories", "controversies", and the like. It is also said that the literary forms of these small units as well as the literary presentation employed in them are found in contemporary Rabbinic and Hellenistic literature. There are also similarities in ideas and content. Hence the conclusion: there must have been borrowing by Christian writers from these sources. Further, only on the supposition that there existed a creative activity in the primitive community can one explain the lack of precision, the loose way of narrating, and the undeniable differences among the Gospels. It is up to the historian, then, to excise by patient analytical labour all that little by little accrued, that is, legendary elements or whatever was added by popular fancy. Above all he must remove elements borrowed from neighbouring religions, known Hellenistic myths about earthly apparitions of the gods, their intervention and involvement in earthly events. Only in this way can one gradually uncover the real historical nucleus of the life of Christ and of his message. Thus what we know historically of both the life and the teaching of Christ is really very little.

As can be seen from this last conclusion, we are dealing

with a type of criticism no less destructive than that of Strauss or Friedrich Christian Baur of the past century. Only the method is different. Even in cases where such extreme conclusions as these are not reached, it often tends to weaken the historical value of the Gospels. It is thus of the utmost importance to get a clear view of the matter.

3. Presuppositions or theoretical postulates of Form Criticism

Let us look, first of all, at the presuppositions or, more exactly, the theoretical postulates of Form Criticism.[1] The first of these postulates is that the material at the source of our Gospels comes from an anonymous primitive community which had no historical interests. This community, precisely because it was carried along by faith, was incapable of taking the position of objectivity which is essential for the

---

[1] The Instruction directs exegetes to use with care the "sound elements" contained in the method of Form Criticism (par. V), and gives two reasons for this. For "scarcely admissible philosophical and theological principles have often come to be mixed with this method, which not uncommonly have vitiated the method itself as well as the conclusions in the literary area. Some proponents of this method have been led astray by the prejudiced views of rationalism. They refuse to admit the existence of a supernatural order and the intervention of a personal God in the world through strict revelation, and the possibility and existence of miracles and prophecies. Others begin with a false idea of faith, as if it had nothing to do with historical truth—or rather were incompatible with it. Others deny the historical value and nature of the documents of revelation almost a priori. Finally, others make light of the authority of the apostles as witnesses to Christ, and of their task and influence in the primitive community, extolling rather the creative power of that community."

The more generic of these reasons will not be discussed here, even though they are often the ultimate root of the difficulty. We shall concentrate rather on the more specific reasons which touch upon the study of the ambient environment in which the Gospel message was spread abroad and the manner of its diffusion. Concerning the more generic presuppositions it will suffice to quote the stern comment of the Instruction, that they "are not only opposed to Catholic doctrine, but are also devoid of scientific basis and alien to the correct principles of historical method" (par. V).

historian; history and faith are incompatible. In addition, this community was creative, that is, it elaborated the material it received—expanding, inventing from its imagination, combining borrowings from the religions of its environment.

Now against these gratuitous affirmations stand the following facts:

The primitive Christian community is not an anonymous community but one which is *well known to us, guided by the apostles* as authorized eyewitnesses.[1] So it appears, in fact, at Jerusalem, where Peter repeatedly preaches as the head of an apostolic college (Acts ii. 14–40; iii. 12–26; iv. 8–12; v. 29–32). He has already acted as the head of that group in the election of a substitute to take Judas' place, even before the Pentecostal descent of the Spirit (Acts i. 15–26). Then, when the good news spreads beyond Jerusalem, the leaders Peter and John go to "inspect" the communities, for instance in Samaria (Acts viii. 14–17). Or Peter alone moves about through the different cities of the Palestinian plain (Acts ix. 32–42). Later Barnabas comes for the same reason to Antioch, having been sent from Jerusalem (Acts xi. 22–3). We are not, then, confronted with the preaching of enthusiasts and fanatics, but with preaching that is well organized and directed by the apostles.

Later on, in his own way, Luke reflects this situation in the introduction to his Gospel. "Inasmuch as many have undertaken to compile a narrative of the things which have been accomplished among us, just as they were delivered to us by

[1] Various aspects of this community have been well presented by C. Martini in "La primitiva predicazione apostolica e le sue caratteristiche", *Civiltà cattolica* 113 (1962–3), 246–55.

those who from the beginning were eyewitnesses and ministers of the word, it seemed good to me also, having followed all things closely for some time past, to write an orderly account..." (Luke i. 1–3). Neither Luke's predecessors nor the evangelist himself made it a rule to cull everything that was recounted in the community about Jesus, but only that which the authorized eyewitnesses had passed on who had become in time the ministers of the word.

From all this it follows that the apostles had a *genuine interest in history*. Obviously they did not intend to write history after the manner of Greek or Roman historiography, that is to say, a history ordered either chronologically or as a chain of cause and effect—history, that is, as an "end in itself". Nevertheless, their interest contained what is essential for any interest in history—the intention to report and faithfully to transmit past deeds and sayings.

A good proof of this is the very notion of "witness", "testimony", or "bearing witness" which in its diverse forms occurs over one hundred and fifty times in the New Testament. For a witness is a person who is in a position to affirm something officially, as it were, on the basis of his own immediate experience. The apostles refer to themselves repeatedly as witnesses of the events of the life of Jesus (Acts i. 22; ii. 32; iii. 15; v. 32; x. 39, 41; xiii. 31; xxii. 15; xxvi. 16; 1 Pet. v. 1). Jesus indeed had said to them before his ascension, "You shall be my witnesses" (Acts i. 8; cf. Luke xxiv. 48). Then in the Cenacle during the period between the ascension and the descent of the Spirit on Pentecost, when the problem of finding a substitute for Judas arose, certain qualities were explicitly required in him. He would have to be a person who had been an eyewitness of the deeds of Jesus "during all the time that the Lord Jesus went in and out among us from the baptism of John until the day that he was taken up from us" (Acts i. 21-2). When St Paul lists for the Corinthians the official witnesses who had seen the risen Lord, he says, "[Christ] appeared to Cephas, then to the Twelve. Then he appeared to more than five hundred brethren at one time, most of whom are still alive, though some have fallen asleep. Then he appeared to James, then to all the apostles . . ." (1 Cor. xv. 5-7).

Yet even if the main *object* of the apostolic *testimony* was the resurrection of Christ, in consonance with its fundamental importance, it was not its sole and exclusive object.[1] On the contrary, the resurrection itself demanded in a very emphatic way the explanation of all that preceded it. For if it really constitutes the supreme glorification of Jesus of Nazareth, it all the more urgently calls for an explanation of his condemnation and death. Indeed, it is well known that the primitive preaching of the apostles pointed to an historical cause of this condemnation and death, ascribing it to the actions of the Jerusalem leaders (see Acts ii. 23; iii. 13, 15; iv. 27; v. 30; x. 39; xiii. 28). But it also proposed a more profound reason, a supernatural one, the fulfilment of the salvific will of God already made manifest in the Scriptures (Acts ii. 23; iii. 18; iv. 28; xiii. 27; 1 Cor. xv. 3). The two causes are intimately connected. A truncated or defective explanation of the events of the historical order would have run the risk at least of creating doubts about the realization of a specific plan of salvation on God's part. For that reason it was necessary to explain not only the facts connected with

[1] Cf. F. Mussner, *op. cit.*, pp. 230-4.

the trial and the death of Jesus, but also those which preceded little by little for the final conflict. It was necessary to expose the occasions and the motives which led up to the conflict itself. Jesus had made claims about his person and his messianic, divine dignity. Statements had been made about the responsibilities of the leaders of the Jews and the future destiny of the people. Finally, the genesis, development and climax of the conflict itself had to be explained. In other words, there had to be an exposition of several points of doctrine intimately connected with the account of the basic facts. This was all the more urgent since Jesus had asserted with considerable emphasis that the Kingdom of God had come with him (Luke xi. 20; Mark i. 15). In using that notable formula, "You have heard that it was said to the men of old . . . but I say to you" (Matt. v. 21), he had contrasted his own person and his teaching with the very foundation of the Mosaic tradition. And yet, his teaching was not just another one of the many traditions passed on to the Chosen People, but rather the teaching of the promised teacher of messianic times.[1]

Finally, from all that has been said it is clear how we must regard the alleged *creative activity* of the primitive community. Let us prescind from the value of the philosophico-sociological theory on which this allegation rests. Today

[1] From this it is apparent what we are to think of the assertion of some Form Critics that faith has no concern for historical truth or that it is actually incompatible with it. We prescind from the case where "faith" is understood in the sense of fiducial faith, as among many Protestants; we understand it in the Catholic sense as an assent to things proposed in preaching. We also leave aside the larger, theoretical question of the nature of faith, since for our present purpose it is certain that the object of faith was intimately connected with the historical facts of the life of Jesus and presupposed them. Faith and history, far from being opposed to one another, rather presuppose and confirm one another mutually. Faith demands and guarantees the maximum of historical truth.

this theory no longer finds the favour among scholars it once did. It is sufficient to recall the facts that have been thus far set forth in order to prove its inaccuracy. For the apostles were authorized witnesses of Jesus and of the events of his life—and not only of the most important events, but also of others intimately connected with them. They witnessed his public life and his preaching.

Moreover, a rather characteristic feature of such preaching was its transmission or "tradition". This involves the ability to receive a teaching, to preserve it, and to pass it on faithfully (cf. 2 Thess. ii. 15; 1 Cor. xi. 2, 23; xv. 1–3; 1 Thess. ii. 13; 2 Thess. iii. 6; Rom. vi. 17; Gal. i. 9, 12; Phil. iv. 9; Col. ii. 6, 8). We should recall above all the well-known formulae of St Paul, "I received . . . what I also passed on to you" (1 Cor. xi. 23); "I passed on to you as of prime importance what I myself received" (1 Cor. xv. 3). Again and again he echoed the advice to preserve the teaching as it had been passed down (2 Thess. ii. 14; 1 Cor. xv. 2; xi. 2). Once he even used a very strong expression in this regard: "Even if we, or an angel from heaven, should preach to you a Gospel contrary to that which we preached to you, let him be damned. As we have said before, so now I say again, If anyone is preaching to you a Gospel contrary to what you have received, let him be damned" (Gal. i. 8–9).

In speaking of such preaching, Paul reports that he went up to Jerusalem "as a result of a revelation", and there laid before them the Gospel that he was preaching among the Gentiles. This he did in private before those who were men of repute, in order to be sure that he "was not running or had run in vain" (Gal. ii. 2). Paul thus refers to the "council" of Jerusalem which is so important for the subject we are discussing. For it was concerned with the controversy which arose over Paul's preaching among the pagans and over the obligations to be imposed on Gentile converts. Various communities of Jewish Christians had been disturbed over this matter because of Paul's preaching. But the controversy in itself shows that the communities exercised a control, one over the other, in the matter of fidelity to the transmission of the Gospel message. The controversy between Paul and the Judaizers was brought before the elders and above all settled by the apostles. The profound significance of this recourse to the apostles and of their intervention is seen in the fact that whether an accusation of infidelity was levelled or a defence was made against such an accusation, there was a common, deep conviction that one must faithfully preserve and pass on unadulterated the received teaching, and that the apostles were to guard over it.[1]

4. *Methods and procedures of Form Criticism*[2]

(*a*) Let us note in the first place a *methodological error* which Form Critics frequently commit in using the comparative history of religions. The argument usually runs as follows.

---

[1] To preserve and to pass on the message in a faithful and unadulterated way does not simply mean a rigid, mechanical transmission. Rather, the intervention of the apostles shows how fidelity in preserving the teaching and in passing it on pure not only does not exclude, but sometimes demands a more profound interpretation of it, so that it can be applied to new cases which come up. We shall speak again of this aspect of transmission later on. What is important now is to affirm the fact of the need to preserve and transmit the teaching faithfully. How it was done will be discussed further on.

[2] The necessary reserves and qualifications which one must make regarding the presuppositions of Form Criticism explain the rather guarded way in which the Instruction of the Biblical Commission speaks of this mode of interpreting the Gospels. It says, "As occasion warrants, the interpreter may examine what sound elements are contained in the Form-Critical method that can be used for a fuller understanding of the Gospels" (par. V). Such reserves and qualifications make it

In the small units shown to exist in the Gospels we find the same literary forms and the same literary presentation as in Rabbinic and Hellenistic literatures; hence we are dealing with elements borrowed from these literatures. Now it is known that the external form of a literary unit is generally dictated by its subject-matter. This is especially true in the Near East, where the same subject-matter is usually treated in quasi-stereotyped terms. Consequently, similarity in literary presentation does not really prove dependence or borrowing, nor does it argue against the truthfulness of the account. For one must attend not only to form but to content as well. When the Gospels are compared with the religions of neighbouring lands, the point which clamours for explanation is the unique element of originality in the Gospel message. It is something for which there is no counterpart either in parallels taken from the religions of the Gospel environment or in parallels taken from religions of other environments. What is more, against the hypothesis of borrowings stands the incontrovertible fact of the apostles' scrupulous care to hand down the deeds and sayings of Christ with fidelity and to see to it that everything be preserved unaltered.

obvious that this way of speaking is quite justified. This is even truer because the Instruction, echoing the Encyclical *Divino afflante Spiritu*, had shortly before recommended rather insistently the use of scientific procedures. These are the result of the progress of science, and Form Criticism makes use of them (but not as of a thing that is exclusively its own). Among the aids furnished to exegesis by such progress the Instruction mentions "above all those which the historical method, taken in its widest sense, offers—a method which carefully investigates sources and defines their nature and value, and makes use of such helps as textual criticism, literary criticism, and the study of languages. The interpreter will heed the advice of Pius XII of happy memory, who enjoined him 'prudently . . . to examine what contribution the manner of expression or the literary genre used by the sacred writer makes to a true and genuine interpretation" (par. IV). We shall have more to say about this topic later.

(*b*) Another methodological procedure used by Form Critics is that of *literary criticism*. Literary criticism has no necessary connection with the gratuitous theoretical postulates discussed above, since it is neither the exclusive patrimony of Form Criticism nor was it invented by it. Form Criticism, it is true, has developed a special way of applying literary criticism to the Gospels, but only after having borrowed this way from various studies of the Old Testament (as was observed earlier) where, moderately, prudently, and soberly employed, it has produced good results. For some time now literary criticism has been widely employed by Catholic exegetes. In their "Introductions" to the individual books of Sacred Scripture they try to illustrate with data *taken from the book in question* the person of the author, his characteristics, his mentality, his style and language, and his purpose. All of these factors are precious data which must be kept in mind by the one who wishes to interpret the book.

The Encyclical *Divino afflante Spiritu* itself deduces the ultimate reason for such a procedure from the fact of inspiration, that is to say from the fact that the human author of a book of the Bible has been employed by the Holy Spirit as a living and intelligent instrument. When an author writes a book under the inspiration of the Holy Spirit, he keeps the full use of his powers and faculties, with the result that all can easily gather from the book produced by his work his distinctive genius and his individual characteristics and features, as Pope Benedict XV indicated in his Encyclical *Spiritus Paraclitus*.[1] For this reason too Pope Pius XII added his exhortation, "Let the interpreter then

[1] *AAS* 12 (1920) 390 (*EB* 448; *RSS* 47).

endeavour with all care and without neglecting any light derived from recent research to determine the distinctive genius of the sacred writer, his condition in life, the age in which he lived, the written or oral sources he may have used, and the literary forms he employed. He will thus be better able to discover who the sacred writer was and what he meant by what he wrote."[1]

(c) A final procedure used by Form Critics is *to determine and to study literary forms*. In this area various proponents of Form Criticism have clearly gone too far in following criteria that were more often than not subjective. It is no wonder, then, that considerable diversity in determining such forms reigns among them. Their classifications, often minutely detailed, seem to correspond more to Hellenistic Greek than to Semitic mentality. It is certainly also an abuse the way some authors have recourse to an alleged literary form in the face of any and every difficulty. Still more objectionable are the tendentious classifications and the use of terms which imply doubt (or worse) about the historical value of the accounts, as, for, example, when they speak of "legends".

And yet neither the excess nor the abuse nor even that degree of uncertainty which inevitably accompanies such study—particularly at the outset—is a reason for condemning the procedure as such.

The existence of definite modes of speaking, narrating, and of teaching which are proper to Sacred Scripture has always been recognized by all who have had any familiarity with the Bible. The meaning of such modes of speaking and of expressing oneself is not always easy to determine. But it

[1] *DaS* 33-4 (*EB* 557; *AAS* 35 [1943] 314; *RSS* 96).

becomes progressively more intelligible as the literature of the ancient Near East comes gradually to light—a process that is as yet far from being finished. Every serious student takes account of this difficulty. Recently the Encyclical *Divino afflante Spiritu* recognized it, saying:

> Frequently the literal sense is not as obvious in the words and writings of ancient oriental authors as it is in the writers of our own time. For what they wished to express is not to be determined by the rules of grammar and philology alone, nor solely by the context. It is absolutely necessary for the interpreter to go back in spirit to those remote centuries of the East, and with the aid of history, archæology, ethnology, and other sciences, determine what literary forms the writers of that ancient period intended to use and did in fact employ.[1]

It is important to note that in speaking of literary forms the Encyclical not only refers to poetry and doctrinal statements, but also to the manner of recounting *facts and historical events*. It is precisely in this very context, in fact, that the Encyclical underlines the singular fidelity to historical truth by which Israel excelled the peoples of the ancient Near East. For the Encyclical adds: "At the same time, no one who has a correct idea of biblical inspiration will be surprised to find that the sacred writers, like any other ancient authors, employ certain fixed ways of exposition and narration, certain idioms especially characteristic of the Semitic languages, so-called approximations and certain hyperbolical expressions and even paradoxical expressions designed for

---

[1] *DaS* 35 (*EB* 558; *AAS* 35 [1943] 314-15; *RSS* 97).

the sake of emphasis."[1] The Encyclical insists that the use of these modes of expression is decidedly not against divine inspiration.[2]

With all these reasons as its basis, the Encyclical *Divino afflante Spiritu* directs a serious exhortation to Catholic exegetes. They must make "prudent use of this means" (i.e. of the study of the literary forms of the Bible), in order to "respond fully to the present needs of biblical science". It further says, "And let him [the exegete] be convinced that this part of his task cannot be neglected without great detriment to Catholic exegesis".[3] One should not miss with regard to this exhortation the new and important specification given to it in the Instruction of the Biblical Commission. If anyone had the impression, for one reason or another, that the principles of the Encyclical *Divino afflante Spiritu* concerning the literary genres of the Bible referred only to the Old Testament, he is informed by the Instruction that this impression is not correct. In this respect the Instruction is evidently providing an authentic interpretation of the encyclical. For it states,

> By this piece of advice Pius XII of happy memory enunciated a general rule of hermeneutics by which the books of the Old Testament as well as the New must be explained. For in composing them the sacred writers employed the way of thinking and writing which was in vogue among their contemporaries (par. IV).

This is a matter of a *general* rule of hermeneutics. Indeed, when there is need of an accurate interpretation—especially

---

[1] *DaS* 37 (*EB* 559; *AAS* 35 [1943] 315; *RSS* 97–8).   [2] *Ibid.*
[3] *DaS* 38 (*EB* 560; *AAS* 35 [1943] 316; *RSS* 98).

in theological matters—every exegete knows what valuable help is derived from the determination or discovery of the mode of speaking, of presenting a maxim, of developing a discussion, or of singling out the precise point towards which the whole passage is converging. This concern for the literary form aids him to discover precisely what the author intended to say. And this is, according to St Athanasius and the Encyclical *Divino afflante Spiritu*, the "supreme rule of interpretation" (*summa interpretandi norma*).[1]

5. Form in which the Gospel message was originally presented and transmitted

With the theoretical presuppositions and procedures of Form Criticism thus clarified we are in a position—as far as one can be within our restricted compass—to answer the questions, "In what forms was the Gospel message originally presented and then transmitted?"

The Instruction gives a directive on this very point. "The exegete will use all the means available to probe more deeply into the nature of Gospel testimony, into the religious life of the early Churches, and into the sense and the value of apostolic tradition" (par. IV). A little further on it undertakes this very task itself, by indicating the general lines of such probing in a way consonant with its purpose. "To judge properly concerning the reliability of what is transmitted in the Gospels, the interpreter should pay diligent attention to the three stages of tradition by which the doctrine and the life of Jesus have come down to us" (par. VI). The three

---

[1] *DaS* 34 (*EB* 557; *AAS* 35 [1943] 314; *RSS* 96).

stages, described in some detail in the rest of the Instruction, are these: (a) what Christ the Lord did in proposing his teaching and educating the apostles; (b) what the apostles did; (c) finally, what the authors of the Gospels did.

The contribution of Jesus, insofar as it pertains to the genesis of the Gospels, is found in his preaching and the instruction given to the apostles that they might be in a position to continue his work. It will be sufficient to cite the short passage of the Instruction itself dealing with this stage of tradition, since different aspects of his work have already been emphasized in the preceding pages, and we can return later to one point or another. The Biblical Commission speaks as follows:

> Christ our Lord joined to himself chosen disciples (Mark iii. 14; Luke vi. 13), who followed him from the beginning (Luke i. 2; Acts i. 21–2), saw his deeds, heard his words, and in this way were equipped to be witnesses to his life and doctrine (Luke xxiv. 48; John xv. 27; Acts i. 8; x. 39; xiii. 31). When the Lord was orally explaining his doctrine, he followed the modes of reasoning and of exposition which were in vogue at the time. He accommodated himself to the mentality of his listeners and saw to it that what he taught was firmly impressed on the mind and easily remembered by the disciples. These men understood the miracles and other events of the life of Jesus correctly, as deeds performed or designed that men might believe in Christ through them, and embrace with faith the doctrine of salvation (par. VII).

As for the second stage of the Gospel tradition, *the contribution of the apostles*, our point of departure is the conclusion reached above, that in the final analysis the Gospels come from the preaching of the apostles, the "ministers of the word" (Luke i. 2). For that reason we must make sure to give a clear picture of that preaching, since its distinctive features will necessarily become part of the Gospels.

(*a*) We recall what has been explained above. Preaching does not mean the drawing up of a complete and chrono-logically ordered "Life of Christ" in the modern sense of the word. This was not the task Christ gave to the apostles. Besides, a very superficial analysis of the Gospels shows at once that this was neither the intention of the authors of the Gospels nor or the apostolic preaching.

And yet, that preaching had an aim which was *funda-mentally historico-biographical*. Not that it intended to compose a biography in our sense of the word, but that it tended to preserve facts about the life of a person, Jesus of Nazareth, facts about his existence and his activity in the context of his teaching.

It is true that in this complex of details the events of the death and resurrection hold the first place—as they are emphasized in the Instruction. But these very events demand an explanation. And this was sought in the deeds of Jesus' public life, in his claims to dignity, and in general in his teaching.

(*b*) This apostolic preaching differed too from ordinary history by the *specific purpose* for which it preserved and handed on the historical facts. It was "preaching", that is to say the proposing and explaining of facts related to *religious instruction* which was to be accepted with faith as man's way to salvation.[1] Now as has already been seen, it is certainly not true that faith and history are incompatible. On the contrary, the faith of the New Testament was precisely of a nature to suppose the historical truth of facts and to base itself upon them. Faith and history do not exclude one another, but the religious aim influenced the *presentation* of the facts, without however changing the facts themselves. This religious purpose required that the facts be explained to one who had not experienced them or who perhaps came from a different environment from that in which the events occurred. The explanation then was given by witnesses who after the descent of the Holy Spirit on the feast of Pentecost were mature in the faith and understood a great many things which they had not understood during the earthly life of Jesus. It was natural for these men to explain things (without altering them) in the light of this more profound understanding of the facts and the doctrine.[2]

[1] In this connection the Instruction says, "From the results of the new investigations it is apparent that the doctrine and the life of Jesus were not simply reported for the sole purpose of being remembered, but were 'preached' so as to offer the Church a basis of faith and of morals" (par. X). But such a purpose would lead to several consequences. First of all, the apostles "faithfully explained his life and words" (par. VIII), but they did so, "while taking into account in their method of preaching the circumstances in which their listeners found themselves" (compare Acts xiii. 16–41 with Acts xvii. 22–31). Moreover, they "preached and made use of various modes of speaking which were suited to their own purpose and the mentality of their listeners. For they were debtors (1 Cor. ix. 19–23) 'to Greeks and barbarians, to the wise and the foolish' (Rom. i. 14)". We shall consider the implications of all this shortly.

[2] The Instruction makes quite a point of this: "There is no reason to deny that the apostles passed on to their listeners what was really said and done by the Lord with that *fuller* understanding which they enjoyed (John ii. 22; xii. 16; xi. 51–2; cf. xiv. 26; xvi. 12–13; vii. 39), having been instructed by the glorious events of the Christ and taught by the light of the Spirit of Truth (John xiv. 26; xvi. 13). So, just as Jesus himself after his resurrection 'interpreted to them' (Luke xxiv. 27) the words of the Old Testament as well as his own (Luke xxiv. 44–5; Acts i. 3), they too interpreted his words and deeds according to the needs of their listeners" (par. VIII).

(*c*) This practical, religious aim had still another consequence. Since it was a matter of "preaching", the facts were clearly not handed on mechanically but rather *in a vital way which corresponded to the character of each preacher*. The various preachers were in agreement on the facts and the substance of what they reported, as was demanded by the exacting responsibility of fidelity to their charge of bearing witness to Christ—to his life, activity, and teaching. But their preaching necessarily differed from preacher to preacher. This was all the more natural since they were eyewitnesses and earwitnesses who were not interdependent. Each was aware of his own previous experience. And it was made up of varying personal observations and varying personal impressions of the person of Jesus, of his deeds and his sayings. This variety was reflected in the preaching. The very *manner of recounting* or explaining things varied according to the different qualities of the speakers' personalities. (How well these features are revealed in the Gospels!) For that reason, even the living "tradition" which the evangelists inherited necessarily had various forms. The comparative study of the synoptic Gospels, carried out in the last decades and extending to the most minute details, shows that one cannot suppose that a *completely uniform* oral tradition underlies the Gospels. In addition to the main lines and the many details on which the evangelists agree, there are perceptible differences in the sayings or deeds narrated as well as in the manner of recounting them.

(*d*) Another characteristic note of this apostolic preaching was that it remained *on the popular level*. This was true not only because its authors (the apostles) were simple folk who were not especially educated, but also because they found their principal audience among people of humble circumstances. Thus one should not expect them to speak about Christ after the manner of an official record obtained from archives. Even less should one expect from them the sort of thing to which modern man is so accustomed, a stenographer's report, or the accuracy of a photograph or tape recording. It is sufficient to recall in this regard the vague nature of the many chronological indications which are contained in the formulae of transition, such as "and then", "on that day", "at that time", etc.[1]

The Instruction, going still further, illustrates the adaptation of the apostles' preaching to its specific purpose and to the mentality of its listeners by enumerating the different ways of proposing the message of Christ which is observed in the Gospels. Account must be taken of these different ways: "catecheses, stories, testimonia, hymns, doxologies, prayers—and other literary forms of this sort which were in Sacred Scripture and were accustomed to be used by men of that time" (par. VIII).

(e) In speaking of the "council" of Jerusalem above, we noted that the faithful preservation and transmission of the teaching of Jesus did not imply a *mechanical* transmission. It was indeed inevitable that in the course of time new cases would be brought up, which had not yet been experienced in precisely that form. In such instances the really faithful preservation of the spirit of the message demanded a more profound meditation on it and an assessment of the circum-

---

[1] See, for instance, the numerous references in A. ROBERT and A. FEUILLET (ed.), *Introduction à la Bible* 2 (Paris, 1959), 164-5, 198.

stances of the case in order that the teaching might be correctly applied to it. Now the religious and didactic purpose of the preaching immediately implied on the part of such a "preacher" a more profound meditation of the message in order to apply it correctly—without any deformation of its sense or content—*to audiences in the different environments* in which he found himself. He did this by applying the teaching to the special needs of the listeners, that is by emphasizing those aspects of the deeds and sayings of Jesus which corresponded to the listeners' needs; or by selecting from the large body of material available to him precisely those deeds and sayings which would clarify or correct the previous religious beliefs of his hearers, root out vices, and encourage them in good and useful tendencies. All this the preacher did by presenting the deeds and sayings in a manner best suited to his aim.

Another quality of this apostolic preaching came from the fact that it was directed to men of the people, to men of little education, and to an environment where *few knew how to write and books were rare*. This circumstance made it necessary to *limit* the teaching to a restricted number of points, *to the essentials, in the manner of a catechism*. It demanded that the explanation be to a certain extent standardized. Mnemonic devices also had to be used in order to help fix events or sayings in the memory. We find in the Gospels mnemonic techniques of composition in the use of the numbers 7, 3, 5, 2. There are instances where various sayings of Christ are linked together by means of catch-words (for example, Mark ix. 33–50; Luke vi. 38a–b). We also find compilations of the discourses of Christ addressed to the people (Matt. v–vii), or to the disciples (Matt. x), as well as groupings of parables (Matt. xiii; Luke iv. 1–34), and miracle stories (Matt. viii–ix), etc.

6. *The function of the evangelists*

The third stage through which the teaching and the life of Jesus passed was that of the commitment of the apostolic preaching to writing. It cannot be doubted that prior to the composition of the four Gospels the preaching of the apostles began to be *fixed in writing*. All this is quite clear; it is deduced from the previously cited text of St Luke in which he says that before him "many have undertaken to compile an account of the events that have happened among us" (Luke i. 1). It follows that prior to our Gospels more or less extensive literary units were in existence. And these sources reproduced the various differences in the apostolic preaching we listed above.

What precisely was *the function of the evangelists* in compiling their books? It is important to get a clear understanding of this. It should not be conceived as the work of a stenographer recording a speech or a sermon. For even if the venerable tradition of the Church states that Mark wrote his Gospel in dependence on the preaching of Peter, and if Luke manifests an affinity with the ideas and preaching of Paul, none of this should be understood in an exclusive sense. Luke himself speaks in general terms of his own toil. Just as others before him undertook to compile an account of the things that happened "among us, as these were passed on to us by those who were eyewitnesses from the beginning and became ministers of the word" (Luke i. 2), so did he too, "having followed up all things closely from the beginning".

The Instruction too is quite explicit and clear in this respect. The evangelists committed to writing, it tells us, the preaching of the apostles "in four Gospels for the benefit of the Churches, with a method suited to the peculiar purpose which each one set for himself. From the many things handed down they selected some things, reduced others to a synthesis, still others they explicated as they kept in mind the situation of the Churches. With every possible means they sought that their readers might become aware of the reliability of those words by which they had been instructed (Luke i. 4)" (par. IX). The function, then, of the evangelists is stated very summarily in the Instruction with these three terms: selection, synthesis, and explication.[1] The criterion and norm which guided their work was the purpose or goal which each evangelist proposed to himself— either the generic purpose that the readers might learn the basis of the apostolic preaching, or the more specific one motivating each of the Gospel writers. But that norm also included a respect for the situation of the readers for whom each evangelist was writing. In this regard the Instruction says:

Indeed, from what they had received the sacred writers above all selected the things which were suited to the various situations of the faithful and to the purpose which they had in mind and adapted their narration of them to the same situations and purpose. Since the meaning of a

[1] Editor's Note: The problematic word *explanantes* in the Latin text of the Instruction is translated in the Italian by *svilupparono*; see *L'Osservatore Romano*, 14 May 1964, p. 3, col. 4. This shows that the sense of *explanare* is not conveyed by the relatively weak English term, "explain". It means rather "unfold, develop, explicate". Cardinal Bea's translation of the three terms: *scegliere, sintetizzare, sviluppare.*

statement also depends on the sequence, the evangelists, in passing on the words and deeds of our Saviour, explained these now in one context, now in another, depending on (their) usefulness to the readers (par. IX).

The Biblical Commission, with its own topic, the historicity of the Gospels, ever before its eyes, adds this important sentence:

The truth of the story is not at all affected by the fact that the evangelists relate the words and deeds of the Lord in a different order, and express his sayings not literally but differently, while preserving their sense (par. IX).

This statement is supported by the authority of two of the greatest exegetes of antiquity, St John Chrysostom and St Augustine.[1]

It is true that the evangelists were faithful to the preaching of the apostles, and to previously existing documents in which their preaching had been set down. But they still had a wide field for their own authentic activity as writers. They had to sift the documents at their disposal, collect the preaching and other testimonies of the apostles still alive, order all this material, and from it construct their book

---

[1] Cf. JOHN CHRYSOSTOM, Hom. in Matt. 1, 2 (PG 57, 16–17); Augustine, De consensu Evangelistarum 2, 12, 28 (PL 34, 1090–1; CSEL 43, 127–9). Here is Augustine's classic testimony: "It is quite probable that each evangelist believed it to have been his duty to recount what he had to in that order in which it pleased God to suggest it to his memory—in those things at least in which the order, whether it be this or that, detracts in nothing from the truth and authority of the Gospel. But why the Holy Spirit, who apportions individually to each one as he wills (1 Cor. xii. 11), and who therefore undoubtedly also governed and ruled the minds of the holy writers in recalling what they were to write because of the pre-eminent authority which the books were to enjoy, permitted one to compile his narrative in this way, and another in that, anyone with pious diligence may seek the reason and with divine aid will be able to find it" (De consensu Evangelistarum 2, 21, 51–2 [PL 34, 1102; CSEL 43, 153]).

according to their own personal conceptions and the needs of their readers. Rightly therefore, even though their dependence on oral and written sources was essential, the evangelists are considered, according to ancient ecclesiastical tradition, *authors* of the Gospels which go by their names.

7. *Conclusion*

The examination of Form Criticism and of the facts which it has brought to light and on which it is based has revealed to us how complex was the reality in which our Gospels took shape. This reality was the living preaching of the apostles, substantially the same in its wide variety of forms, and the documents in which it was fixed prior to the Gospels.

Realization of this complexity serves at once as a warning against a characteristic tendency of modern man: the desire to solve all problems overnight. He is easily led to forget tradition and, in an impossible effort to solve personally all problems, to ignore what has been achieved and to jettison the most elementary certitudes. What is required then is rather a cautious and patient labour distinguishing what is certain and solid from what really needs further study and re-examination. In his wild haste modern man forgets that things of the spirit cannot be treated like material things; they require time for reflection and mature judgement. Otherwise, hasty and erroneous solutions to problems lead to a terrible loss of time and energy. The serious consequences of such haste are in fact to be seen in Form Criticism and especially in its extreme forms, such as "demythologization". Therefore no one should rush rashly into this type of study if he is not properly trained, especially in sound theology. And even with such training one must proceed with great patience and reflection, never losing sight of the tradition and teaching of the Church.

If, then, the reality in which our Gospels took shape was very complex, it is not for that reason less solid. It is not lost in a vague, hazy, and uncertain obscurity. Quite the contrary. Our explanation has revealed the solid basis of our Gospels, "the truth of the teaching" (Luke i. 4) which we have received. What is reported rests on the solid rock of the testimony of "the ministers of the word"—a testimony which, notwithstanding the variety of presentation, agrees not only in the larger, over-all picture, but even in many details. This testimony is worthy of our acceptance, even when there are divergences, provided that we look at them not with the mentality of today but with the patient effort of one who seeks to transfer himself to the time of the authors, to their mentality, and to their way of speaking.

Thus far we have been considering the Gospels from a purely human and historical point of view. We have not taken into account inspiration and therefore we have not asserted the absolute inerrancy of the Gospels although this is their privilege, because they are not only human works, but also and principally the work and the word of God himself. Whoever considers them in this way, as every Catholic exegete must, is confronted with still further problems. These we shall consider in the following chapter.

II

The historical character of the
Synoptic Gospels considered
as inspired writings

At the conclusion of the last chapter, in which we commented on the recent Instruction of the Biblical Commission, we indicated the particular problem which we would take up here. It is the problem of understanding how the historical character of the Gospels is affected by the fact that their principal literary author is God himself. For from this fact one concludes that the Gospels enjoy not only a genuine historical credibility in what they affirm and in the way in which they affirm it, but also that perfect form of it which is called inerrancy. For God, being absolute Truth, cannot err or utter anything but the truth. This is why the Instruction urges the exegete never to forget "that the Gospels were written under the inspiration of the Holy Spirit, who preserved their authors from all error" (par. XI).

And yet, there are many verses in the Gospels where—at least at first sight—one is left perplexed. In such instances the ordinary reader, and even the specialist and exegete, asks again and again, "How is it possible that such and such a thing would be inspired? To what extent is inerrancy involved here." Let us take up some of these problems. And first of all, in a general way.

A certain overly abstract view of biblical inerrancy can convey the idea that it demands that different authors who report the same event should do so in exactly the same way, since, after all, truth is one. When such statements are made, those who make them are probably thinking of philosophical formulations, or at least of purely theoretical enunciations of truth. Again, concern for biblical inerrancy can make a person overly sensitive about the differences which exist among the Gospels so that he shies away from them.

But common sense suggests at once that clear distinctions be made between the differences that exist among the evangelists. Here are some examples of such differences, arranged in a scale of ascending difficulty. It is certainly surprising that the Sermon on the Mount is set in different contexts by Matthew and Luke. Moreover, Matthew enumerates eight beatitudes, while Luke gives only four, but adds to them the "Woes" (cf. Matt. v. 3–10; Luke vi. 20–6). More difficult is the case of the differences in the account of the healing of the centurion's servant. In Matthew it seems that the centurion himself came to Jesus, while in Luke the centurion sends the elders of the Jews, explicitly saying that he is not worthy to meet the Master. And as a matter of fact, according to Luke he does not meet our Lord (Matt. viii. 5–13; Luke vii. 1–10). But if one is justified in general in regarding Matthew (differently from Mark and Luke) as providing schematic accounts of the miracles, what is to be said of the differences in the text of the *Our Father*, as it appears in Matthew and Luke (Matt. vi. 9–13; Luke xi. 2–4)? Or of differences in words so unique and so important as those of the institution of the Eucharist (Matt. xxvi. 26–8; Mark xiv, 22–4; Luke xxii. 19–20)?

In the face of such facts different *attitudes* can be assumed. There is first the attitude of those who do not pay sufficient attention to what inerrancy implies and so fail to take into account its range and the difference existing between it and the fidelity to be expected of a work that is merely human. Others are so disturbed by these differences in the Gospels that they cannot calmly look the facts in the face. They prefer to ignore the results of scientific research and the progress of modern methodology. Finally there is the attitude of those who carefully unite in their efforts both fidelity to biblical inerrancy and a wise and prudent use of the solidly established results of scientific exegesis.

It is this last approach which we are describing in this chapter. We shall seek above all to deepen our understanding of the mystery of inspiration itself in an effort to learn, as it were from inside, the positions which may be adopted in principle in reconciling the inspiration and the consequent inerrancy of the sacred books with the differences among sacred authors writing of the same things. We shall then examine the various kinds of differences, and see why they exist. Finally we shall present some principles which should govern the attitude of Catholics who are confronted with such difficulties—in particular exegetes, professors, and preachers. This last point is treated more fully in the Instruction of the Biblical Commission and it will be discussed especially in the light of the Instruction.

1. *The inspiration of the sacred books and its consequences for the inspired authors' manner of writing*

The Encyclical *Divino afflante Spiritu*, speaking of the difficulties and questions raised in our times about the interpretation of the Bible, admits that our modern age has "also provided, by God's favour, new means and aids for exegesis. Deserving special mention among these is the fact that Catholic theologians, following the teaching of the Fathers and in particular of the Angelic and Common Doctor, have examined and explained the nature and effects of biblical inspiration more precisely and more fully than was customary in previous ages."[1] The salient feature of this new exposition is undoubtedly the doctrine of instrumentality. This doctrine teaches that in producing a sacred book the Holy Spirit does not use the author as a secretary to whom he dictates; nor does he simply reveal to the human author the contents of the book and the way in which this should be expressed. Rather, the human author is, though "truly an instrument" of the Holy Spirit, "a living instrument, endowed with reason", who "under divine impulse brings his faculties and powers into action in such a way that all can easily gather from the book produced by his work his distinctive genius and his individual characteristics and features."[2] In other words, the sacred author employs all his faculties—his intellect, imagination, and will—no less than any other human author. At the same time, however, he is subject to a special influence of the Holy Spirit. While

[1] *DaS* 33 (*EB* 556; *AAS* 35 [1943] 314; *RSS* 96).
[2] *Ibid.* Pius XII here cites Benedict XV, *Spiritus Paraclitus* (*EB* 448; *AAS* 12 [1920] 390; *RSS* 47).

this influence permits the author the full use of all his faculties, it brings it about with the ease proper to divine omnipotence that the author writes exactly that which the Spirit of God wills, only that which he wills, and in the way in which he wills."[1]

The immediate *consequence* of the doctrine on instrumentality is what the same Encyclical calls *the divine condescension*. This means that "in Scripture divine things are presented to us in a manner which is in common use among men. For as the substantial Word of God made himself like to men in all things 'except sin' (Heb. iv. 15), so God's words, spoken by human tongues, have taken on all the qualities of human language except error. This is that condescension of our provident God, which St John Chrysostom praised so highly and which, he repeatedly asserted, can be found in the sacred books."[2]

A corollary of this is the general principle which the same Encyclical enunciates as follows: "Of those ways of speaking which were in use among the ancients, especially the Orientals, to express in human language the conceptions of the mind, not one is alien to the sacred books, provided only that the way of speaking employed does not contradict the holiness of God or the truth."[3]

But at once *the question* comes up: Can these principles be applied to the Gospels? The Gospels certainly are inspired. Still, by their very nature, their exposition and their narratives, they depend directly on "witnesses foreordained by God", the apostles, and follow the apostolic sources with the greatest fidelity, as we have. Now it is true that though

---

[1] LEO XIII, *Providentissimus Deus* (EB 125; ASS 26 [1893–4] 288–9; RSS 24).
[2] *DaS* 37 (EB 559; AAS 35 [1943] 316; RSS 98).   [3] *Ibid.*

the apostles preached, filled with the Holy Spirit, yet they did not preach under the influence of the charism of inspiration. This is indeed true, but the evangelists, in assuming into their works the preaching of one or more of the apostles, did so under divine inspiration. Thus the apostolic preaching which entered into the Gospels and in the form in which it entered the Gospels became inspired. Therefore everything we have said above about inspiration and its consequences applies to the Gospels.

Now if the subject matter of the Gospels is presented in a way to which men are accustomed, and if we are trying to understand, as it were from inside, the causes of the differences among the evangelists, we must study *the human way of narrating in general and that of the Orientals in particular.* And that is precisely what *Divino afflante Spiritu* exhorts Catholic exegetes to do:

> Hence the Catholic commentator, in order to comply with the present needs of biblical studies, in explaining the Sacred Scripture and in demonstrating and proving its immunity from all error, should also make a prudent use of this means, and determine to what extent the manner of expression or the literary mode adopted by the sacred writer may lead to a correct and genuine interpretation. Let him be convinced that this part of his task cannot be neglected without serious detriment to Catholic exegesis.[1]

As we have said in the first chapter, just as some techniques of Form Criticism have been misused, so the deter-

---

[1] *DaS* 38 (*EB* 560; *AAS* 35 [1943] 316; *RSS* 98).

mination of literary genres can also be abused. These tools are very delicate and in using them there is danger of rash or subjective judgements. But this is no reason to condemn and to reject the tools themselves.

2. *Psychological reflections on the manner of narrating and presenting an event*

(*a*) In the previous chapter we discussed the forms in which the Gospel message was presented to us. We also mentioned several reasons why, in spite of fidelity to the truth, some differences were to be expected in the Gospels in the manner in which they presented the Gospel message. Let us recall those reasons briefly.

First of all, we noted that the Gospels resemble "preaching" rather than the accounts which are found in official documents or archives. They convey an "announcement", a proclamation, an exposition, and religious instruction designed to win the living consent of faith from men for their salvation. Obviously the preaching corresponded to the character of each preacher and varied with it, especially when each preacher relied on his own *personal observation*, which differed considerably from the observations of others.

Next, this preaching was popular in character, directed as it was principally to simple people. Finally, the accounts were always adapted to the needs of the hearers both with regard to the choice of facts and the way of presenting them.

(*b*) To probe still more deeply into the sources of the differences, let us turn to some considerations of a general psychological nature which concern the way human beings normally perceive, observe, and present what has been perceived.[1]

(i) The first consideration is concerned with the *completeness of human observation*. It starts with the well-known and statistically certified fact that the ordinary man, not especially trained as an observer, succeeds in grasping about 12 per cent of any given fact or event. The trained observer, such as a policeman or detective, perceives a maximum of 36 per cent. This is the source of great difficulties in the law courts, even aside from all deliberate and emotional deformation or hiding of the truth. So we may ask: Does an account based on such necessarily incomplete observations by that very fact sin against the truth? Certainly men do not ordinarily think so. Provided that the person telling the story intends to affirm only what he has actually seen and heard, he cannot be accused of lying. True, the account is incomplete, fragmentary, open to further completion, but strictly speaking

---

[1] These remarks are based on the obvious data of the common experience of men, quite apart from any theory. This is all the more necessary because, as far as we can tell, scientific research has not yet progressed very far in the psychological study of how people observe and how they recount their experiences. The following titles, however, may be consulted: C. L. MUSATTI, *Elementi di psicologia della testimonianza* (Padua, 1931); F. GORPHE, *La critique du témoignage* (Paris, 1927); R. WOODWORTH and H. SCHLOSBERG, *Experimental Psychology* (New York, 1958), "Retention", p. 724, col. 2; O. KLINEBERG, *Psychologie sociale* (Paris, 1957), "La mémoire", pp. 1,246 ff.

We may note in passing a certain parallel which exists between our approach and that of some Form Critics. They regard the Gospels as "creations" of an anonymous primitive community. So they study the psychology of popular environment, which is the usual setting for the birth of legends. In contrast, we have shown (in the first chapter) that the essential function of the apostles was that of witnesses pre-ordained by God and preachers of the Good News. Hence it is our task now to study the psychology of such preachers, of their preaching, and the various aspects of their activity.

it cannot be called false.[1] Photographic exactness is certainly not the only "true" way of recording events. And if a human way of reporting events is not contrary to truth, then, according to the principles of God's condescension exposed above, neither is there any reason to exclude it from Holy Scripture, and hence from the Gospels. It will be the task of the exegete to discover both what the writer intended to say and the way in which he said it; otherwise we might be led to consider as erroneous a report which is only incomplete.

We have thus indicated a first source of possible differences or lack of harmony in the preaching of the various apostles and in the Gospels, differences which can be admitted without difficulty. These can be of such a kind that the various accounts complete one another (in this case there is no special difficulty). But they can also give the appearance of contradiction, insofar as we may be unable to see positively how the accounts can be harmonized. The classic example of this is provided by the different accounts of our Lord's apparitions after his resurrection. These accounts confirm the well-known psychological principle that the more we have to do with moving events which excite the onlooker, the more difficult it is to preserve accuracy of observations.[2]

(ii) The consideration of the incompleteness of observation must now be continued by a discussion of *the way in*

---

[1] We may make this statement quite apart from any theoretical explanation, basing our judgement simply on the fact that men in general do not regard such behaviour as a violation of the truth. If this were the case, then who would ever be able to relate the simplest story with a clear conscience?

[2] There is obviously no question here of cases of diseased or abnormal excitement, as is supposed in some theories which consider the apparitions of the risen Christ as hallucinations of the witnesses, including the apostles. What we are supposing is the excitement which is understandable and quite normal in the face of such extraordinary events.

which facts, personally observed or learned from others, are narrated. Let a number of people observe the same event and then give their account of it. What a number of instructive results will appear! One person will deliver himself of a few words, giving a mere skeleton-account of the event, but at the same time noting the essential and principal elements. Another will provide an abundance of details, though perhaps without stressing the essential features very clearly. One man's approach will be rather abstract, another's will be concrete or even dramatic. Different details will be stressed.

In this matter we can learn much from St Augustine, who in his work *De Consensu Evangelistarum* struggled so hard to find a solution, at least in principle, to many of these problems which still bother us today (though they were posed in a form and mode different from ours). Dealing with the question about the actual words employed by John the Baptist at the baptism of Our Lord—those reported by Matthew or those reported by Luke (Matt. iii. 7–12; Luke iii. 7–9)—Augustine replies that it is not really necessary to know this. The important thing is to know the *thought* which the Precursor expressed.

> It is clear that each of them [the evangelists] has given an account according to his recollection of the event, and according to his judgement as to how it should be proposed, either briefly or in detail; but there is always the same thought.

The Holy Doctor continues by saying that the divine authority of the Gospels

> forbids us to think that any of the evangelists could speak untruly, even when the same event is narrated by different

individuals and in different words. Thus the evangelists may change the order of events; they may prefer one mode of expression to another (provided that these have the same meaning); they may, while clearly recalling the event itself, not succeed, despite their effort to do so, in preserving the exact words which were spoken on the occasion.[1]

But all the differences noted do not proceed solely from habits of observation or from memory. They are also due to the narrative ability, which in turn depends on the character, imagination, etc. of the person concerned. We need only consider the obvious case of different preachers who want to utilize, for instance in a catechism lesson, the same "example" in order to illustrate their doctrine. Let us suppose something that often happens. The example is not taken from something personally seen or observed by the preacher, but from

---

[1] 'Ut enim quisque meminerat, et ut cuique cordi erat vel brevius vel prolixius eandem tamen explicare sententiam, ita eos explicasse manifestum est. Et in hoc satis apparet, quod ad rem maxime pertinet, quoniam veritas evangelii verbo Dei, quod supra omnem creaturam aeternum atque incommutabile permanet, per creaturam temporalibus signis et linguis hominum dispensato summum culmen auctoritatis obtinuit, non nos debere arbitrari mentiri quemquam, si pluribus rem, quam audierunt vel viderunt, reminiscentibus, non eodem modo atque eisdem verbis eadem tamen res fuerit indicata, aut sive mutetur ordo verborum, sive alia pro aliis, quae tamen idem valeant, verba proferantur ... sive rem bene tenens non assequatur, quamvis id conetur, memoriter etiam verba, quae audivit, ad integrum enuntiare" (De Cons. Evang., 2, 12, 27–8; PL 34, 1090–1; CSEL 43, 127–128).

St Augustine then makes the following characteristic remark: If anyone should claim that the power of the Holy Spirit ought to have helped the evangelists not to differ in their choice of words, the ordering of the words, or the numbers of the words, then he simply does not understand that this procedure of the evangelists was quite necessary if they were to persuade other men of their veracity. There can be no question of lying where many people describe the same event but differ from one another in their manner of expression. In other words, the truth is in no wise violated if the same events are narrated in different ways and with different words. It follows from what we have said above about the divine "condescension" that this procedure is quite admissible in Sacred Scripture, and thus in the Gospels.

a book. What a variety of presentations is possible while still keeping the substantial reality of the fact! The variety will be greater still if the congregations to which the lesson is addressed are of different types. Adults will need a presentation different from that suitable to children. The same applies to groups of people with greater or less education.

Common sense requires that we admit that these differences *as such* (that is, with these limits) in no wise offend against the truth. Otherwise who would ever dare to include such examples in his sermons or catechetical instructions? He would suffer from endless scruples, thinking that he was constantly sinning against the truth.[1] It follows then that such differences are perfectly admissible in the sacred book itself, in the preaching of the apostles and in the Gospels. We can expect great variety in the various accounts and this is in perfect harmony with inerrancy and with fidelity to what the Master did and taught.[2]

(iii) It is important also to consider, when discussing the Gospels, that we are not dealing with observers or narrators of our own times who reflect in their activity the psychology of the modern West. On the contrary, we are dealing with an ancient world whose culture and mentality were essentially simpler, and so to speak more primitive, than ours. For such men the imagery of figures and metaphors was

[1] We shall discuss later the deeper reason underlying this judgement of common sense when we come to explain the importance and function of the writer's intention (see p. 63).

[2] It is proper to recall what the Instruction of the Biblical Commission says of the work of the evangelists and what we considered in the last chapter. That is, out of all the material which they had at their disposal they selected what was adaptable to the diverse conditions of the faithful and to the aim which they (the evangelists) had in mind. Other things they worked into a synthesis; still others they unfolded and developed, as they kept in mind the concrete situations of the individual churches.

more important than it is for us. The Encyclical *Divino
afflante Spiritu* notes that in the sacred writers "certain fixed
ways of exposition and narration are found, certain idioms
which belong particularly to Semitic languages, so-called
approximations and certain hyperbolic expressions and even
paradoxical expressions which serve to impress more deeply
on the mind what the writer wants to say".[1] We have seen
in the preceding chapter how the Instruction insists that all
of this is not only true in general but also valid for the
Gospels. Admittedly, it is harmful to exaggerate such
peculiarities in Oriental style, as though it had nothing in
common with the psychology of the West; but it is equally
harmful to neglect it.

(iv) Up to now we have been supposing that different
witnesses *narrate the same fact*. But in the Gospels we often
have reason to ask if the evangelists are always really dealing
with the same event. This may appear to be a mere subter-
fuge to get rid of difficulties, but this is not so. Let us recall
that the apostles spent *at least* a year and a half[2] in the school
of their divine Master. They were his companions on many
journeys and heard many of his long and unforgettable
sermons. These sermons came back again and again to the
same essential themes, but they also varied according to the
people who heard them—according to their mentality,
culture, etc. Now it is a well-known fact that in such
repetitions small variations are wont to appear even though

---

[1] *DaS* 37 (*EB* 559; *AAS* 35 [1943] 315; *RSS* 97–8). Cf. also the Response of the
Biblical Commission to Cardinal Suhard, 16 January 1948 (*EB* 581; *AAS* 40 [1948]
47; *RSS* 150–1).
[2] A more exact determination of the length of the public life of Jesus (and hence
of the duration of the formation of the apostles by him) is a subject of debate
among the exegetes; opinions vary from one to three years.

the same fundamental themes are being presented. Different images and comparisons are introduced according to the different groups of hearers; sometimes the stress is on the intellect, sometimes on the imagination. Thus the apostles, in their preaching, had a very rich and varied source to draw on. It follows, then, that in many cases it is at least legitimate to ask if we are really dealing with the same deed or word of Christ when we find two or more evangelists differing slightly in their account of it.[1]

(c) Let us conclude our discussion of the psychological factors which could have influenced the way in which facts are narrated and events are presented in the Gospels. Divine inspiration does not exclude any literary procedure in legitimate usage among men, that is any mode of expression which does not run counter either to truth or God's holiness. But, as a matter of fact, this human usage is far from excluding variety in its way of speaking about the same subject, whether it be an event or a point of doctrine; on the contrary such *variety is natural and inevitable*. In keeping with differences of personality and character there will be differences in observing, narrating, and presenting facts. This phenomenon is of course accentuated when we move from one ethnic group to another, and still more from one race to another. In addition, differences such as these find stronger expression when we are dealing with popular cultures which retain with greater spontaneity the characteristic features of their origins in psychology, in self-expression, and in language.

Far from being surprised or astounded, we should find

---

[1] In these cases recourse is often too easily had to doublets. Thus unnecessary problems are created about the differences between the Gospels in their recording of the "same" saying of Christ.

such differences perfectly natural, even in the Bible. What is more, we even gain by these differences. If the apostles had not furnished us with a message which varied in the aspects of the mystery which it presented and in matters of emphasis and style, we might well ask why Christ chose twelve apostles so different in temperament, as the Gospels reveal them. But as a matter of fact, we know that Christ wanted the infinite light of his life and doctrine to come to us through the lives, the characters, and the teaching of the apostles. It is like the light of the sun broken down by the prism into all the colours of the spectrum and revealed in all its richness. In the Encyclical *Humani generis* Pius XII noted that the doctrine revealed to us by God is so rich that it can never be exhausted.[1] The same is obviously true of Christ who is at once divine and human, as well as of his life and activity. When confronted with this complex reality, every human being realizes his own limitations and must therefore admit the limitations of all that he can say or write about him or his work, no matter how sublime his language may be.

St Augustine makes this remark in speaking of the "eagle" among the evangelists, St John:

I venture to say, brethren, that not even John himself has presented these things just as they are, but only as best he could, since he was a man who spoke of God—inspired, of course, but still a man. Because he was inspired he was able to say something; but because he who was inspired remained a man, he could not present the full reality, but only what a man could say about it.[2]

---

[1] *EB* 611; *AAS* 42 (1950) 568; NCWC Engl. tr. (1950), p. 10, # 21.

[2] *In Ioannem*, tract. 1, 1 (*PL* 35, 1379–80; *Corpus Christianorum*, ser. lat. 36, 1).

This is the reason why our Lord wished that twelve apostles should speak of himself to us, that they might complement one another's work and that their testimony might be not only more reliable but also richer, and as far as possible, exhaustive.

3. *Attitudes towards the differences among the Gospels*

These differences have their use and even their advantages, but this does not prevent their causing the interpreter many a headache. However, the Encyclical *Divino afflante Spiritu* forewarns us that we are not to be frightened or discouraged by difficulties. In natural and profane investigations one gathers fruit only after much labour. The same is true in the study of the faith, according to the Encyclical—which goes on to add a thought dear to the Fathers of the Church and especially to St Augustine. It was God's wish that the Bible "should have difficulties scattered through it so that we might be spurred on to read and study it with greater diligence and thus realize our own limitations and be exercised in due humility".[1] This leads to the important conclusion that we should make sure at every point that we assume a proper attitude towards these difficulties lest we err either against faith, or the truth and inerrancy of Sacred Scripture, or against humility and prudence.

(*a*) *Above all, the faith.* Since we know with the certitude of faith that we are dealing with books which are the word and work of God who cannot err, why then should we be upset by every difference or lack of harmony which we

---

[1] *DaS* 45 (*EB* 563; *AAS* 35 [1943] 318; *RSS* 101).

encounter in the Gospels? This is a sign of insecure faith,
Faith forbids us to doubt about the divine character and the
inerrancy of the Bible, even when we meet obscurity and
human limitations in it. Provided that they in no wise
conflict with the truth or with the holiness of God, they have
been expressly permitted by God, through his divine
condescension, to be in his inspired word. We would do well
to recall the famous saying of Leo XIII with regard to
conflicts of faith and science: "Truth can never contradict
truth."[1] And this is so in our case too. Seeing that all four
Gospels are the word of God, it is impossible for them to
contain real contradictions. Let us endeavour then to explain
the differences which we note and solve the problems
which they raise, but let us do this with peace of mind.

(b) More specifically, we should point out *one attitude that
ought not be adopted* in our attempts to resolve the problems
in question. One cannot be content with this attitude: "It is
enough to get to the essentials, the religious element, that
which concerns faith and morals; everything else in the
Gospels can be considered as the trappings in which the
religious teaching is clothed." Underlying this distinction is
the following reasoning. The aim of the sacred authors is
properly a religious and moral one. It is this element alone
which they wish to affirm. The rest is not part of what the
sacred authors affirm, and hence does not come under
inerrancy.

What is to be said of such reasoning? Apart from the fact
that it presents in a new form doctrines previously con-

[1] *Providentissimus Deus* (EB 131; ASS 26 [1893-4] 291; RSS 27): "Verum vero
adversari haudquaquam potest."

demned,[1] this argument is a hasty oversimplification. First of all, it is not as easy as we sometimes think to distinguish what concerns faith and morals from the rest of the Bible. This is particularly so since in Christian faith it is *not abstract principles and theoretical doctrine* that are of primary importance but rather facts: the history of God's saving acts carried out with humanity and in humanity. Further, these facts are for the most part interconnected, like the stones of a building. If one or other stone is moved, the whole structure begins to shake. This method also runs the risk of overlooking certain facts and details simply because the exegete for the moment does not see their connection with faith and morals or with the essentials of faith. And yet these points may really be much more important than they seem.

(c) Here are *some of the principal rules* for a positive approach to this difficulty.

(i) One can never insist enough on the fact that we must be wary of our peculiarly modern mentality and must therefore never equate the Gospel text either with a stenographer's record or a transcription of a sermon registered on

---

[1] It is in fact difficult to see how this opinion escapes the condemnation of *Providentissimus Deus*, which was directed against those who restrict inspiration merely to matters of faith and morals (cf. *EB* 124; *RSS* 24. The same notion is found in *Humani generis*, ≠ 22; *EB* 612; NCWC Engl. tr., p. 11). It is true that in this opinion it is not inspiration that is being restricted, but rather the *intention* of the sacred writer. But even this view is almost verbatim excluded by the same encyclical, which rejects the view that "when there is question of the truth of statements, one should not consider so much what God has said as to weigh the reason why he has said it" (*Providentissimus Deus, EB* 124; *RSS* 24). However, this difference should be noted, that the Encyclical speaks of the intention of the *primary* author, while in the view we are discussing it is a question of the intention of the human author (or "hagiographer"). Let us add, finally, that the question, "What is the intention of the author?" is in itself not to be condemned. It is indeed of capital importance, as we shall see later. But what is to be criticized is the hasty and over-simplified manner of determining this intention, when one limits it without further ado to religious matters.

tape. As for the narratives, we should never interpret them as documents preserved in archives or "reports" in the modern sense of the word. Nor should we look on them as chronicles. We should not expect of the Gospels either the modern ideal of accuracy or the exactitude of explicit citations set off between quotation marks.

(ii) It is most important, therefore, that we ask ourselves on every occasion: *what was the intention of the author?* What exactly did he want to say, assert or affirm? The principle is well known that whatever the sacred author asserts or affirms must be considered as asserted and affirmed by the Holy Spirit himself, and therefore as infallibly true. Our fundamental question then is: what does the author concretely want to say, assert or affirm? To seek the answer to this question is "the supreme rule of interpretation".[1]

We shall illustrate the importance of this principle with an example. Earlier we spoke about a preacher who uses the same example in order to illustrate a point of doctrine in a sermon to children, to adults, to a group of intellectuals, or to a congregation of ordinary people. Why do we instinctively consider as legitimate all the variations which characterize the different presentations *of the same example* and the appreciable differences in the various accounts—differences which we never consider to be a distortion of the truth? Because we instinctively realize what the *preacher wishes to say exactly* and distinguish it from the concrete expressions which he employs. We realize that the preacher does not wish to maintain that every small detail which he uses occurred exactly as he expresses it. He uses in his account to little children (who are incapable of sustained attention)

---

[1] *DaS* 34 (*EB* 557; *AAS* 35 [1943] 314; *RSS* 96).

many picturesque details in order to capture their imagination. He is simply using a lively manner of presenting the substance of his message to this specific category of hearer. This distinction between the vivid presentation and the substance of the message is made by us all the more spontaneously, if we know the preacher to be particularly lively.[1]

Now when we apply all this to the Gospels, let us remember that we are dealing with an inspired evangelist. It is well to recall *the insistence of the Biblical Commission's Instruction*. It recommends repeatedly to the exegete that he investigate what was *the intention of the evangelist* in proposing a saying or an event in a given context. It also adds the caution that if the exegete does not make use of all that recent studies have contributed, "he will not fulfil his task of probing into what the sacred writers intended and what they really said" (par. X). We shall find this intention, then, by employing the usual means known to every interpreter. These include the comparison of the compositions of the evangelists with one another, the determination of the literary form actually employed and the laws which govern it, and the study of the modes of speaking (about which we shall speak shortly).

The Gospel writers themselves are not the only ones who must be considered. In the first chapter we noted that the preaching of some of the apostles, or a part of their preaching, had been put in writing in other documents before they were finally taken up into our Gospels. The evangelists did not always have first-hand knowledge of the apostles'

---

[1] This distinction is not to be confused with the one mentioned above, between the moral-religious scope of the author and everything else. According to the distinction which we are now making, we must hold as true *all* that the sacred author asserts and affirms, whether he is speaking of religious and moral matter or of others.

preaching and they certainly used such documents. These they duly sifted under the influence of the charism of inspiration which preserved them from error.[1] Having assured themselves of the authenticity and accuracy of the documents, they used them with reverence and care. Therefore when we succeed by means of literary criticism in identifying these documents or parts of such documents in the Gospel texts, we must ask the following question: "What was the intention of the person who composed those documents?" or, "What was the intention of the apostle whose preaching was set down in that document?" This is certainly a work which demands great patience and reflection to ensure that we do not fall victim to our own subjective impressions, but at the same time it is a most necessary and rewarding work.

(iii) Again, we must take into account and study carefully *the mode of expression and of telling a story* which was characteristic of the ancient Orient in general. Insofar as it is possible, we must study the mode of expression of the individual authors, including the apostles to whom one or other of the Gospels is attributed.[2]

First of all, the way of speaking and of recounting characteristic of the *ancient Orient in general*. There is a manner of narration which indeed has a genuinely historical preoccupation, and yet the only thing that matters in it is the thought contained in the statement. This manner of narration may be presumed, provided that in some way or other, for example from the customary usage of the milieu, we can

---

[1] Cf. *Humani generis* 38 (*EB* 618; *AAS* 42 [1950] 576–7; NCWC Engl. tr., pp. 17–18).

[2] For instance, one thinks readily of the style of Matthew and of the vivid way of narrating which characterizes Mark's Gospel.

determine that the author was presenting only the thought. Besides this, there is also the manner of recounting a fact either with greater amplitude than is strictly required or only schematically.

Thus the Encyclical *Divino afflante Spiritu*, speaking of this very question, that is, of the manner of narrating historical facts, has no difficulty in admitting "approximations and certain hyperbolic expressions"[1] in the Bible. It further adds:

> In effect, when some people presume to accuse the sacred authors of an historical error or inaccuracy in the recording of facts, it is often found to be merely a question of those customary ways of speaking and recounting which the ancients commonly used in their mutual dealings with one another, ways which were considered quite licit and acceptable. When therefore such ways are found in Scripture, which was written for men in human language, it is only right that they be no more branded as errors than they would be if used in the ordinary intercourse of daily life.[2]

(iv) A word, now, about *the way in which the words of Jesus are transmitted to us in the Gospel*. Here one can fall into error very easily, either by considering every saying without distinction as an exact, literal quotation, or by going to the other extreme, especially in cases where the words resemble each other but differ on certain points, of concluding too rapidly that "evidently" there is question of the *same* saying of Jesus which has been reported by two sources only accord-

---

[1] *DaS* 37 (*EB* 559; *AAS* 35 [1943] 315; *RSS* 98).

[2] *DaS* 39 (*EB* 560; *AAS* 35 [1943] 316; *RSS* 98). See also the Response of the Biblical Commission to Cardinal Suhard, 16 January 1948 (*EB* 581; *AAS* 40 [1948] 47; *RSS* 150-1).

ing to its basic sense. To follow the proper course in this matter, regard must be had both for those factors which favour an exact and uniform record and those which favour the existence of variations. Considering the matter *from the standpoint of Christ* himself, we must say that he certainly must have repeated many times over the same truth with the same incisive formulae. His purpose was to inculcate his doctrine when speaking in public or else to fix it in the minds of the apostles.[1] This was actually the traditional method among the Rabbis, the only one available at a time when the use of books or scrolls was rare and difficult.[2] The rhythmic formulas and mnemonic sentences still found in the Gospels testify to the use of this method.[3] Christ himself must have found it necessary to vary his presentation from time to time either to hold the interest of his audience or to illustrate the truth of his words with different images and comparisons from diverse points of view.

From the apostles' point of view there was, as a result of the education given them by Christ, the tendency to report

[1] Recall that passage of the Biblical Commission's Instruction, which was already discussed in the first chapter (p. 34), where it is said that Jesus "saw to it that what he taught was firmly impressed on the mind and easily remembered by the disciples" (par. VII).

[2] It is not possible to go into details in this matter. The interested reader can consult B. GERHARDSSON, *Memory and Manuscript: Oral Tradition and Written Transmission in Rabbinic Judaism and Early Christianity* (Acta seminarii neotestamentici Upsaliensis 22; Uppsala, 1961); H. SCHÜRMANN, "Die vorösterlichen Anfänge der Logien-Tradition. Ein Versuch eines formgeschichtlichen Zugangs zum Leben Jesu", in H. RISTOW and K. MATHIAE (ed.), *Der historische Jesus und der kerygmatische Christus* (Berlin, 1960), pp. 342–70, esp. pp. 362–70. Editor's note: An extended summary of Gerhardsson's book can be found in my article, "Memory and Manuscript: The Origins and Transmission of the Gospel Tradition", *Theological Studies* 23 (1962), 442–57. See also the review of P. BENOIT, *Revue biblique* 70 (1963), 269–73. Gerhardsson's book evoked a mixed reaction among reviewers, and he answered the negative criticism of it in "Tradition and Transmission in Early Christianity", *Coniectanea neotestamentica* 20 (1964).

[3] See Chapter I, p. 39.

verbatim (*ad verbum*) what he had said, although we cannot attribute to them the fidelity of a stenographer. Because memory was involved variations would be inevitable in the selection of this or that saying. In addition, since the apostles had heard many sermons of Christ, one of them would have been more impressed with one formulation, another with another, and thus different formulations would arise. And a third would even combine two or more variant formulations.[1]

What has been said of the tendency towards uniformity regarding the apostles applies as well to the *disciples of the apostles*, before the preaching was crystallized in the canonical Gospels. As a result of their training they tended to report events verbatim (*ad verbum*) but with the possibility of slight variations in the choice of one or other word.

Considering all the important factors which favour the tendency to report *ad verbum*, it is easy to see that the number of sayings reported in this way, or almost entirely in this way, is not small. Consequently, we need not exaggerate the number and importance of sayings reported in other ways.[2]

---

[1] In what has already been said the main lines of the solution have been indicated for the problem of the way in which the *Our Father* and the words of institution of the Eucharist are reported in the Gospels. Limitations of space do not permit us to go into great detail about this.

[2] From this it should be evident how we are to react towards the unprecise and exaggerated ways of speaking encountered at times. For instance, anyone who seriously reflects on the statement often heard that not all the sayings attributed to Jesus in the Gospels can in fact be considered as his will easily perceive how many distinctions have to be made in understanding it. For if this statement means that not all the sayings recorded in the Gospels as utterances of Jesus were literally pronounced by him precisely as recorded, the statement is not saying anything new. A comparison of the Gospels, one with the other, shows only too clearly that their authors often reported the sayings of Jesus according to their sense, and not with literal fidelity. If then they can differ in the transmission of such unique words as those with which Jesus instituted the Eucharist at the Last Supper (compare Matt. xxvi. 26–8; Luke xxii. 19–20; 1 Cor. xi. 24–5), and again those of the *Our Father*

(v) One last rule. When we apply the principles of literary criticism to the Gospels, and establish that there were blocks or sections of matter existing independently before being incorporated into a Gospel by an evangelist, and when we distinguish by this means between what is more primitive and immediate in an account from what is a later explanation furnished by the apostles or by the evangelist for the benefit of a specific public or audience, we sometimes give the impression that we are establishing two or three categories of texts or textual elements which theologically possess *different values*. These procedures of literary criticism are certainly important for the determination of the intention of

(Matt. vi. 9–13; Luke xi. 2–4), and do not quote him literally or verbatim, how much truer this must be in the case of his many other sayings!

In this connection we should recall again the words of St Augustine which were already quoted: the thought-content is much more important than the verbatim saying (see pp. 54–5 above). In another place he adds this noteworthy observation: "Let us not think [that it is an advantage for our faith to know all these things], as if the truth were somehow bolstered up by set and consecrated words (*consecratis sonis*), or as if God were entrusting to us not only the thing itself, but also the words which were used about it. Rather, the thing which is learned is so much more to be preferred that we should not seek after those words (*istos* [*sonos*]) at all, if we could know it without them, as God knows it, and as his angels know it in him" (*De consensu evangelistarum*, 2, 66, 128; *PL* 34, 1139; *CSEL* 43, 231).

On the other hand, if that often heard statement is supposed to mean that it is doubtful whether Jesus *ever* said the thing, not even in different words or in another context, and *the thought* is attributed to him by the Gospels, then this statement certainly offends against the inerrancy of the Gospels.

It is likewise a mistake to conclude from the fact of the Gospel differences that we do not know at all what Jesus said. As a matter of fact, even if the formula of the institution of the Eucharist does vary from evangelist to evangelist, and from the Gospels to St Paul, there are common elements in all three, and these are of no little moment. It can, therefore, be admitted that we do not know *the literally exact words* pronounced by Jesus on that occasion—but not that we do not know at all what he said. Though one seeks to get as close as possible to the original formula of institution, one should also imitate the example of the Church which has culled the formula from all these words for the Canon of the Mass in a spirit of profound veneration. Why? Because she was certain that they are all the word of God and so constitute the unique means by which the Spirit of God and of Christ guides and introduces us to the entire truth!

the author and for the interpretation of the texts. This interpretation will vary with different authors, and with the different intentions of the same authors. But these procedures must not give rise to confusion as if what is less primitive has less *theological* value, is any less the word of God, is less genuine or less faithful to the thought of Christ, etc. Such an opinion might seem plausible to one who considers the Gospels purely from the viewpoint of human history. But one who considers them as the inspired word of God cannot hold such an opinion. For as the word of God, the Gospels contain all the guarantees of being an authentic and valid instrument by means of which the Holy Spirit himself "guides us into the full truth" (John xvi. 13), into the genuine thought of Christ.

4. *The tasks of different groups in the Church engaged in the interpretation of the Gospels*

Having discussed the problem of the historicity of the Gospels, the Biblical Commission in its Instruction turns its attention to the practical side of the issue. It provides a summary outline of what the Church expects in this matter from those who deal with the Gospels in some official capacity. The guiding principle in this part of the Instruction is that the Gospels are not only a subject to be studied, but the very foundation of the Church's faith and of man's salvation. All Gospel study and research should therefore be ultimately aimed at this. Respect for this principle is the supreme rule in treating the Gospels, whether in research, in teaching in seminaries, in popular instruction, or in publication. Like a wire conductor, this principle unites the recommendations made to the different groups.

(*a*) To "those whose task it is to teach in seminaries and similar institutions" the general principle once formulated by Pius X is again proposed: "Their 'prime concern [should be] that ... Holy Scripture be so taught as both the dignity of the discipline and the needs of the times require' " (par. XII).[1] More specifically, the Instruction recalls the exhortation of the Encyclical *Divino afflante Spiritu*, that such teachers are to pay attention above all to the theological teaching of the Gospels as the source of the spiritual life and of preaching. They are to give first place to the theological values of Scripture, that it "may become for the future priests of the Church both a pure and never-failing source for their own spiritual life, as well as food and strength for the sacred task of preaching which they are about to undertake".[2] A practical rule is then deduced from all this, namely, that literary criticism should not be treated as an end of Scripture intended by God.

When they practice the art of criticism, especially so-called literary criticism, let them not pursue it as an end in itself, but that through it they might more plainly perceive the sense intended by God through the sacred writer. Let them not stop, therefore, halfway, content only with their literary discoveries, but show in addition how these things really contribute to a clearer understanding of revealed doctrine, or, if it be the case, to the refutation of errors. Instructors who follow these norms will enable

[1] Apostolic Letter *Quoniam in re biblica* (EB 162; RSS 36).
[2] *DaS* 55 (EB 567; *AAS* 35 [1943] 322; RSS 104).

their students to find in Sacred Scripture that which can "raise the mind to God, nourish the soul, and further the interior life" (par. XII).[1]

(*b*) The same recommendation to be concerned with the "doctrine" of Scripture is extended to "those who instruct the Christian people in sacred sermons". The Instruction continues (par. XIII):

Let them above all pass on doctrine, mindful of St Paul's warning: "Look to yourself and your teaching; hold on to that. For by so doing you will save both yourself and those who listen to you" (1 Tim. iv. 16).

Prudence is especially recommended to the preachers. This is applied especially to their use of new opinions and interpretations.

They are to refrain entirely from proposing vain or insufficiently established novelties. As for new opinions already solidly established, they may explain them, if need be, but with caution and due care for their listeners. When they narrate biblical events, let them not add imaginative details which are not consonant with the truth (par. XIII).

The application of prudence is obviously not to be understood in any exclusive sense. There are as many ways of applying it as there are different situations, circumstances of person and place, and difficulties which arise. We add here one remark which should be taken to heart especially by preachers, but also by others. It has to do with the highly

---

[1] *DaS* 25 (*EB* 552; *AAS* 35 [1943] 311; *RSS* 93).

desirable use of *the greatest precision in speech*. For so much of the confusion among listeners and readers, perhaps the bulk of it, is due to a lack of precision and prudence in formulation.

An example or two. The facile statement is often made that there are "contradictions" or something similar in the Gospels, when we are really confronted with details that are mutually complementary. Or else it is a question of details which seem to us to be contradictory, because we do not see how we should combine them in one account (as we have already mentioned above). So, for example, in the accounts of the appearances of Christ after his resurrection. Or again, where we have several accounts of one and the same event, one is schematic, and because of its brevity leaves itself open to being understood in various ways or even to being misunderstood, while the other is a richly detailed account.[1]

In such cases it is possible to be confronted with what seems to be a *material* contradiction—as far as the wording goes. Take, for instance, the well-known recommendation of Jesus that the disciples practice complete poverty on their preaching mission and trust in divine providence. According to Matt. x. 10 and Luke ix. 3; x. 4 the apostles are to take along neither staff nor shoes; but according to Mark vi. 8 ff. they may take them. In such cases interpreters must look for the exact sense of the absolute prohibition. Is not Mark giving the *sense* of Christ's words according to the true intention of the Master (Mark in fact is using indirect speech)? On the other hand, Luke may be picturing Christ using hyperbole or paradox "to impress the thought more

[1] The classic example, discussed long ago by St Augustine and others, is that of the cure of the centurion's servant (Matt viii. 5–13; Luke vii. 1–10).

deeply on the mind", knowing that he would not be mis-understood, since both Jesus and the apostles actually wore sandals according to Palestinian custom. In other words, we are dealing with a way of speaking. When this is explained, the apparent contradiction is resolved.

(c) The need to insist on the theological teaching of Scripture and on prudence has made the Biblical Commission come back again to these points in addressing "those who publish for the faithful" (par. XIV). Prudence must ever be the characteristic of this group. The Instruction continues:

> Let them carefully bring forth the heavenly riches of the divine word "that the faithful . . . may be moved and inflamed rightly to conform their lives to them".[1] They should consider it a sacred duty never to depart in the slightest degree from the common doctrine and tradition of the Church. They should indeed exploit all the real advances of biblical science which the diligence of recent students has produced. But they are to avoid entirely the rash remarks of innovators.[2] They are strictly forbidden to disseminate, led on by some pernicious itch for newness, any trial solutions for difficulties without a prudent selection and serious discrimination, for thus they perturb the faith of many (par. XIV).

If the grave urgency of such prudence in dealing with the faithful is not appreciated, it would not be out of place to recall how St Paul wrote to those Corinthian Christians who thought that they could eat the food sacrificed to idols

---

[1] *DaS* 50 (EB 566; *AAS* 35 [1943] 320; *RSS* 103)
[2] Apostolic Letter *Quoniam in re biblica* 13 (EB 175; *RSS* 38)

without any regard for the weak consciences of those who were scandalized at such eating.

> Take care that this right of yours does not become a stumbling-block for the weak . . . In sinning against your brothers in this way and in wounding their weak consciences, you are really sinning against Christ (1 Cor. viii. 9, 12).

5. Conclusion

Our exposé of the complex problem of the historicity of the Gospels has shown, we hope, how dense and compact the recent Instruction of the Biblical Commission is, and how important it is. It has also indicated how justified one of the concluding statements addressed to the exegetes is.

> There are still many things, and of the greatest importance, in the discussion and explanation of which the Catholic exegete can and must freely exercise his skill and genius so that each may contribute his part to the advantage of all, to the continued progress of sacred doctrine, to the preparation and further support of the judgement to be exercised by the ecclesiastical magisterium, and to the defence and honour of the Church (par. XI).[1]

The complexity of the problem also makes clear "how necessary and important the Church's interpretation is" (par. X). This is why the Instruction, after having spoken of the tasks which call for the free exercise of the skill and genius of the exegete, urges him to "be disposed to obey the magisterium of the Church" (par. XI).

[2] Compare the text of DaS 47 (EB 565; AAS 35 [1943] 319; RSS 102).

Fully cognizant of the grandeur and the importance of the exegetes' tasks, the Biblical Commission expresses in the very introduction of its Instruction its great satisfaction that there are many sons of the Church who are devoting themselves to these tasks with wholehearted dedication.

It is a source of great joy that there are found today, to meet the needs of our times, faithful sons of the Church in great numbers who are experts in biblical matters. They are following the exhortations of the Supreme Pontiffs and are dedicating themselves wholeheartedly and untiringly to this serious and arduous task (par. II).

To ensure the calm and serene progress of such work, the Instruction stresses emphatically the *spirit* in which it should be carried out. The words of Pope Leo XIII are once again quoted:

Care should be had that the keen strife of debate should never exceed the bounds of mutual charity. Nor should the impression be given in an argument that truths of revelation and divine traditions are being called in question. For unless agreement among minds be safeguarded and principles be carefully respected, great progress in this discipline will never be expected from the diverse pursuits of so many persons (par. II).[1]

Charity and respect are especially required for those exegetes who are hardy pioneers and who enter a terrain encumbered with difficulties, fully aware of their risk. In this connection the Instruction recalls the grave admonition of

[1] Apostolic Letter *Vigilantiae* (EB 143; RSS 33).
[2] DaS 47 (EB 564; AAS 35 [1943] 319; RSS 101).

the Encyclical *Divino afflante Spiritu*.[2] "Let all the other sons of the Church bear in mind that the efforts of these resolute labourers in the vineyard of the Lord are to be judged not only with equity and justice, but also with the greatest charity" (par. II). And a rather significant motive is added for this respect: "Since even illustrious interpreters, such as Jerome himself, tried at times to explain the more difficult questions with no great success" (par. II).[1]

There is no doubt that the Instruction, with the doctrinal clarification it offers and the spirit which it inculcates, is perfectly suited to bring forth a efflorescence of studies in the Gospels. And these studies will result in the Gospels being pondered, meditated, and preached with increased love and fervour, as they become ever more and more the source of the renewal of the Church in Christ.

[1] Cf. Benedict XV, *Spiritus Paraclitus* 2, 3 (*EB* 451; *AAS* 12 (1920) 392–3; *RSS* 50).

Appendix

Instruction concerning the historical truth of the Gospels[1]

I. Holy Mother the Church, "the pillar and bulwark of truth",[2] has always used Sacred Scripture in her task of imparting heavenly salvation to men. She has always defended it, too, from every sort of false interpretation. Since there will never be an end to (biblical) problems, the Catholic exegete should never lose heart in explaining the divine word and in solving the difficulties proposed to him. Rather, let him strive earnestly to open up still more the real meaning of the Scriptures. Let him rely firmly not only on his own resources, but above all on the help of God and the light of the Church.

[1] Editor's Note: This translation of the Instruction first appeared in *Theological Studies* 25 (1964) 402–8 and is reproduced here with the kind permission of the editors of that review. It is based on the Latin text of the Instruction which was published in *L'Osservatore Romano*, 14 May 1964, p. 3, and later in *AAS* 56 (1964) 712–18. This translation preserves the paragraphs of the original. The italics too reflect those of the original, so that the structure of the document indicated by them should be evident. Certain paragraphs in the Latin text were marked with Arabic numerals. But the principle underlying their use changes after a while, so that they are not a good guide to the structure of the Instruction. In order to facilitate reference to the text, we have added Roman numerals to all the paragraphs of the Instruction. The numbering of the footnotes of the Latin text is generally preserved; occasionally it has been necessary to reverse two of them because of the English wording. For some strange reason the references to the Encyclical *Divino afflante Spiritu* are given in the Latin text of the Instruction to the Italian translation of the Encyclical in *AAS*; we have changed them to the corresponding pages of the official Latin text. Words added in parentheses in this translation do not appear in the Latin text, but are supplied for the sake of the English.

[2] 1 Tim. iii. 15.

II. It is a source of great joy that there are found today, to meet the needs of our times, faithful sons of the Church in great numbers who are experts in biblical matters. They are following the exhortations of the Supreme Pontiffs and are dedicating themselves wholeheartedly and untiringly to this serious and arduous task. "Let all the other sons of the Church bear in mind that the efforts of these resolute labourers in the vineyard of the Lord are to be judged not only with equity and justice, but also with the greatest charity",[1] since even illustrious interpreters, such as Jerome himself, tried at times to explain the more difficult questions with no great success.[2] Care should be had "that the keen strife of debate should never exceed the bounds of mutual charity. Nor should the impression be given in an argument that truths of revelation and divine traditions are being called in question. For unless agreement among minds be safeguarded and principles be carefully respected, great progress in this discipline will never be expected from the diverse pursuits of so many persons."[3]

III. Today more than ever the work of exegetes is needed, because many writings are being spread abroad in which the truth of the deeds and words which are contained in the Gospels is questioned. For this reason the Pontifical Biblical Commission, in pursuit of the task given to it by the Supreme Pontiffs, has considered it proper to set forth and insist upon the following points.

IV. 1. Let the Catholic exegete, following the guidance of the Church, derive profit from all that earlier inter-

---

[1] *DaS* 47(*EB* 564; *AAS* 35[1943] 319; *RSS* 101).
[2] Cf. *Spiritus Paraclitus* 2, 3 (*EB* 451; *RSS* 50).
[3] Apostolic Letter *Vigilantiae* (*EB* 143; *RSS* 33).

preters, especially the holy Fathers and Doctors of the Church, have contributed to the understanding of the sacred text. And let him carry on their labours still further. In order to put the abiding truth and authority of the Gospels in their full light, he will accurately adhere to the norms of rational and Catholic hermeneutics. He will diligently employ the new exegetical aids, above all those which the historical method, taken in its widest sense, offers to him—a method which carefully investigates sources and defines their nature and value, and makes use of such helps as textual criticism, literary criticism, and the study of languages. The interpreter will heed the advice of Pius XII of happy memory, who enjoined him "prudently . . . to examine what contribution the manner of expression or the literary genre used by the sacred writer makes to a true and genuine interpretation. And let him be convinced that this part of his task cannot be neglected without serious detriment to Catholic exegesis."[1] By this piece of advice Pius XII of happy memory enunciated a general rule of hermeneutics by which the books of the Old Testament as well as the New must be explained. For in composing them the sacred writers employed the way of thinking and writing which was in vogue among their contemporaries. Finally, the exegete will use all the means available to probe more deeply into the nature of Gospel testimony, into the religious life of the early Churches, and into the sense and the value of apostolic tradition.

V. As occasion warrants, the interpreter may examine what sound elements are contained in the "Form-Critical method" that can be used for a fuller understanding of the

[1] *DaS* 38 (*EB* 560; *AAS* 35 [1943] 316; *RSS* 98).

Gospels. But let him be wary, because scarcely admissible philosophical and theological principles have often come to be mixed with this method, which not uncommonly have vitiated the method itself as well as the conclusions in the literary area. For some proponents of this method have been led astray by the prejudiced views of rationalism. They refuse to admit the existence of a supernatural order and the intervention of a personal God in the world through strict revelation, and the possibility and existence of miracles and prophecies. Others begin with a false idea of faith, as if it had nothing to do with historical truth—or rather were incompatible with it. Others deny the historical value and nature of the documents of revelation almost *a priori*. Finally, others make light of the authority of the apostles as witnesses to Christ, and of their task and influence in the primitive community, extolling rather the creative power of that community. All such views are not only opposed to Catholic doctrine, but are also devoid of scientific basis and alien to the correct principles of historical method.

VI. 2. To judge properly concerning the reliability of what is transmitted in the Gospels, the interpreter should pay diligent attention to the three stages of tradition by which the doctrine and the life of Jesus have come down to us.

VII. *Christ our Lord* joined to himself chosen disciples,[1] who followed him from the beginning,[2] saw his deeds, heard his words, and in this way were equipped to be witnesses of his life and doctrine.[3] When the Lord was orally explaining his doctrine, he followed the modes of reasoning and of exposition which were in vogue at the time. He

[1] Mark iii. 14; Luke vi. 13.   [2] Luke i. 2; Acts i. 21–2.
[3] Luke xxiv. 48; John xv. 27; Acts i. 8; x. 39; xiii. 31.

accommodated himself to the mentality of his listeners and saw to it that what he taught was firmly impressed on the mind and easily remembered by the disciples. These men understood the miracles and other events of the life of Jesus correctly, as deeds performed or designed that men might believe in Christ through them, and embrace with faith the doctrine of salvation.

VIII. *The apostles* proclaimed above all the death and resurrection of the Lord, as they bore witness to Jesus.[1] They faithfully explained his life and words,[2] while taking into account in their method of preaching the circumstances in which their listeners found themselves.[3] After Jesus rose from the dead and his divinity was clearly perceived,[4] faith, far from destroying the memory of what had transpired, rather confirmed it, because their faith rested on the things which Jesus did and taught.[5] Nor was he changed into a "mythical" person and his teaching deformed in consequence of the worship which the disciples from that time on paid Jesus as the Lord and the Son of God. On the other hand, there is no reason to deny that the apostles passed on to their listeners what was really said and done by the Lord with that fuller understanding which they enjoyed,[6] having been instructed by the glorious events of the Christ and taught by the light of the Spirit of Truth.[7] So, just as Jesus himself after his resurrection "interpreted to them"[8] the words of the Old Testament as well as his own,[9] they too interpreted his words and deeds according to the needs of their listeners. "Devot-

---

[1] Luke xxiv. 44–8; Acts ii. 32; iii. 15; v. 30–2.   [2] Acts x. 36–41.
[3] Compare Acts xiii. 16–41 with Acts xvii. 22–31.
[4] Acts ii. 36; John xx. 28.   [5] Acts ii. 22; x. 37–9.
[6] John ii. 22; xii. 16; xi. 51–2; cf. xiv. 26; xvi. 12–13; vii. 39.
[7] John xiv. 26; xvi. 13.   [8] Luke xxiv. 27.   [9] Luke xxiv. 44–5; Acts i. 3.

ing themselves to the ministry of the word",[1] they preached and made use of various modes of speaking which were suited to their own purpose and the mentality of their listeners. For they were debtors[2] "to Greeks and barbarians, to the wise and the foolish".[3] But these modes of speaking with which the preachers proclaimed Christ must be distinguished and (properly) assessed: catecheses, stories, testimonia, hymns, doxologies, prayers—and other literary forms of this sort which were in sacred scripture and were accustomed to be used by men of that time.

IX. This primitive instruction, which was at first passed on by word of mouth and then in writing—for it soon happened that many tried "to compile a narrative of the things"[4] which concerned the Lord Jesus—was committed to writing by the *sacred authors* in four Gospels for the benefit of the Churches, with a method suited to the peculiar purpose which each one set for himself. From the many things handed down they selected some things, reduced others to a synthesis, (still) others they explicated as they kept in mind the situation of the Churches. With every (possible) means they sought that their readers might become aware of the reliability[5] of those words by which they had been instructed. Indeed, from what they had received the sacred writers above all selected the things which were suited to the various situations of the faithful and to the purpose which they had in mind, and adapted their narration of them to the same situations and purpose. Since the meaning of a statement also depends on the sequence, the evangelists, in passing on the words and deeds of our

---

[1] Acts vi. 4.   [2] 1 Cor. ix. 19–23.   [3] Rom. i. 14.
[4] Luke i. 1.   [5] Luke i. 4.

Saviour, explained these now in one context, now in another, depending on (their) usefulness to the readers. Consequently, let the exegete seek out the meaning intended by the evangelist in narrating a saying or a deed in a certain way or in placing it in a certain context. For the truth of the story is not at all affected by the fact that the evangelists relate the words and deeds of the Lord in a different order,[1] and express his sayings not literally but differently, while preserving (their) sense.[2] For, as St Augustine says, "It is quite probable that each evangelist believed it to have been his duty to recount what he had to in that order in which it pleased God to suggest it to his memory—in those things at least in which the order, whether it be this or that, detracts in nothing from the truth and authority of the Gospel. But why the Holy Spirit, who apportions individually to each one as he wills,[3] and who therefore undoubtedly also governed and ruled the minds of the holy (writers) in recalling what they were to write because of the pre-eminent authority which the books were to enjoy, permitted one to compile his narrative in this way, and another in that, anyone with pious diligence may seek the reason and with divine aid will be able to find it."[4]

X. Unless the exegete pays attention to all these things which pertain to the origin and composition of the Gospels and makes proper use of all the laudable achievements of recent research, he will not fulfil his task of probing into what the sacred writers intended and what they really said.

---

[1] Cf. John Chrysostom, *Hom. in Matth.* 1, 3 (*PG* 57, 16–17).
[2] Augustine, *De consensu Evangelistarum* 2, 12, 28 (*PL* 34, 1090–1; *CSEL* 43, 127–9).
[3] 1 Cor. xii. 11.
[4] *De consensu Evangelistarum* 2, 21, 51–2 (*PL* 34, 1102; *CSEL* 43, 153).

From the results of the new investigations it is apparent that the doctrine and the life of Jesus were not simply reported for the sole purpose of being remembered, but were "preached" so as to offer the Church a basis of faith and of morals. The interpreter (then), by tirelessly scrutinizing the testimony of the evangelists, will be able to illustrate more profoundly the perennial theological value of the Gospels and bring out clearly how necessary and important the Church's interpretation is.

XI. There are still many things, and of the greatest importance, in the discussion and explanation of which the Catholic exegete can and must freely exercise his skill and genius so that each may contribute his part to the advantage of all, to the continued progress of sacred doctrine, to the preparation and further support of the judgement to be exercised by the ecclesiastical magisterium, and to the defence and honour of the Church.[1] But let him always be disposed to obey the magisterium of the Church, and not forget that the apostles, filled with the Holy Spirit, preached the good news, and that the Gospels were written under the inspiration of the Holy Spirit, who preserved their authors from all error. "Now we have not learned of the plan of our salvation from any others than those through whom the Gospel has come to us. Indeed, what they once preached they later passed on to us in the Scriptures by the will of God, as the ground and pillar of our faith. It is not right to say that they preached before they had acquired perfect knowledge, as some would venture to say who boast of being correctors of the apostles. In fact, after our Lord rose from the dead and

[1] *DaS* 47 (*EB* 565; *AAS* 35 [1943] 319; *RSS* 102).

they were invested with power from on high, as the Holy
Spirit came upon them, they were filled with all (his gifts)
and had perfect knowledge. They went forth to the ends of
the earth, one and all with God's Gospel, announcing the
news of God's beauty to us and proclaiming heavenly peace
to men."[1]

XII. 3. Those whose *task it is to teach in seminaries and
similar institutions* should have it as their "prime concern
that . . . Holy Scripture be so taught as both the dignity of
the discipline and the needs of the times require".[2] Let the
teachers above all explain its theological teaching, so that the
Sacred Scripture "may become for the future priests of the
Church both a pure and never-failing source for their own
spiritual life, as well as food and strength for the sacred task
of preaching which they are about to undertake".[3] When
they practice the art of criticism, especially so-called literary
criticism, let them not pursue it as an end in itself, but that
through it they might more plainly perceive the sense
intended by God through the sacred writer. Let them not
stop, therefore, halfway, content only with their literary
discoveries, but show in addition how these things really
contribute to a clearer understanding of revealed doctrine,
or, if it be the case, to the refutation of errors. Instructors
who follow these norms will enable their students to find in
Sacred Scripture that which can "raise the mind to God,
nourish the soul, and further the interior life".[4]

XIII. 4. Those *who instruct the Christian people in sacred*

---

[1] Irenaeus, *Adversus haereses* 3, 1, 1 (Harvey 2, 2; *PG* 7, 844).
[2] Apostolic Letter *Quoniam in re biblica* (*EB* 162; *RSS* 36).
[3] *DaS* 55 (*EB* 567; *AAS* 35 [1943] 322; *RSS* 104).
[4] *DaS* 25 (*EB* 552; *AAS* 35 [1943] 311; *RSS* 93).

sermons have need of great prudence. Let them above all pass on doctrine, mindful of St Paul's warning: "Look to yourself and your teaching; hold on to that. For by so doing you will save both yourself and those who listen to you."[1] They are to refrain entirely from proposing vain or insufficiently established novelties. As for new opinions already solidly established, they may explain them, if need be, but with caution and due care for their listeners. When they narrate biblical events, let them not add imaginative details which are not consonant with the truth.

XIV. This virtue of prudence should be cherished especially *by those who publish for the faithful*. Let them carefully bring forth the heavenly riches of the divine word "that the faithful . . . may be moved and inflamed rightly to conform their lives (to them)".[2] They should consider it a sacred duty never to depart in the slightest degree from the common doctrine and tradition of the Church. They should indeed exploit all the real advances of biblical science which the diligence of recent (students) has produced. But they are to avoid entirely the rash remarks of innovators.[3] They are strictly forbidden to disseminate, led on by some pernicious itch for newness, any trial solutions for difficulties without a prudent selection and serious discrimination, for thus they perturb the faith of many.

XV. This Pontifical Biblical Commission has already considered it proper to recall that books and articles in magazines and newspapers on biblical subjects are subject to the authority and jurisdiction of ordinaries, since they treat of religious matters and pertain to the religious instruction of

---

[1] 1 Tim. iv. 16.   [2] *DaS* 50 (*EB* 566; *AAS* 35 [1943] 320; *RSS* 103).
[3] Apostolic Letter *Quoniam in re biblica* 13 (*EB* 175; *RSS* 38).

the faithful.[1] Ordinaries are therefore requested to keep watch with great care over popular writings of this sort.

XVI. 5. Those who are in charge of biblical associations are to comply faithfully with the norms laid down by the Pontifical Biblical Commission.[2]

XVII. If all these things are observed, the study of the Sacred Scriptures will contribute to the benefit of the faithful. Even in our time everyone realizes the wisdom of what St Paul wrote. The sacred writings "can instruct (us) for salvation through faith in Christ Jesus. All Scripture is divinely inspired and profitable for teaching, for reproof, for correction, and for training in uprightness, so that the man of God may be perfect, equipped for every good work".[3]

XVIII. The Holy Father, Pope Paul VI, at the audience graciously granted to the undersigned secretary on 21 April 1964, approved this Instruction and ordered the publication of it.

Rome, 21 April 1964

BENJAMIN N. WAMBACQ, O.PRAEM.
Secretary of the Commission

---

[1] Instruction *De consociationibus biblicis* . . . (*EB* 626).
[2] *Ibid.* (*EB* 622-33).   [3] 2 Tim. iii. 15-17.

List of Abbreviations

AAS   *Acta Apostolicae Sedis.*

ASS   *Acta Sanctae Sedis*

CSEL *Corpus Scriptorum Ecclesiasticorum Latinorum* (Vienna).

DaS   The Encyclical *Divino afflante Spiritu.*

EB   *Enchiridion Biblicum* (4th ed.; Rome and Naples, 1961).

PG   Migne, *Patrologia Graeca.*

PL   Migne, *Patrologia Latina.*

RSS   *Rome and the Study of Scripture* (5th ed.; St. Meinrad, Ind., 1953).

Index

A

Apostles: filled by Holy Spirit in their preaching, 15, 86–7; authorized eyewitnesses concerned for historical truth, 22–4, 26; historical accuracy needed for their testimony, 24–5; their contribution to tradition of Gospel message, 34 ff; their preaching historico-biographical, 35; concerned with religious instruction, 35–6, 85–86; their contribution based on personal experience and observation, 37; their preaching essentially popular, 37–8; and adapted to the needs of their hearers, 38–9

Athanasius, St, 33

Augustine, St, 42 and n, 60; *De Consensu Evangelistarum*, 42n, 54–5, 55n, 69n, 85n; *In Joannem*, 59 and n

B

Bea, Cardinal A., 7–8, 41n

Benedict XV: *see Spiritus Paraclitus*

Benoit, P., 17n, 67n

C

Chrysostom, St John, 42 and n, 49, 85n

D

De consociationibus biblicis, 89n

Delorme, J., 7n

Descamps, A., 17n

Divino afflante Spiritu: as *magna charta* of biblical studies, 11; principles for interpretation of Gospels, 13; support for literary criticism, 29–30, 30n; attitude towards question of literary forms, 31–3, 81 and n; and new aids to exegesis, 48 and n; and the doctrine on instrumentality, 49 and n, 50 and n, 81 and n; and figures of speech, 57 and n; and attitude to exegetical difficulties, 60 and n; and intention of author, 63n; and manner of narration, 66 and n; exhortation to seminary teachers, 71 and n, 72 and n, 87 and n; on free exercise of exegetical skill, 75n, 86n; support for pioneer exegetes, 76 and n (80n)

Dodd, C. H., 17n, 18n

E

Eucharist, institution of, 15, 68–9n

Evangelists: their part in the tradition of the Gospel, 34, 40 ff; not stenographers, 40; their principles of selection, 41–2, 42n, 84–5; were authors in their own right, 42–3; necessity of investigating intention of, 64–5, 85–6; and their modes of expression, 65

F

Fitzmyer, J. A., (editor), 8n
Florit, E., 17n
Form Criticism: creates a twofold problem, 14–16; calls historicality and inspiration of Gospels in question, 14–16; aims at explaining origins of Gospels, 17; its sources, 17–18; and literary forms, 17–18; faith and history incompatible, 19, 22; and *Sitz im Leben*, 18; care needed in using its method, 21n, 32–3, 81–2; and comparative religion, 27; its scientific method recommended by Instruction, 27–8n, 81–2; the use it makes of literary criticism, 29–30; its study of literary forms, 30–3; has helped to reveal complexity of origins of Gospels, 43; and "demythologization", 43

G

Galbiati, E., 7n
Gerhardsson, B., 67n
Gorphe, F., 52n
Gospels: exposed to alterations and intrusions, 14; their historical value in question, 14ff; their inspiration and inerrancy presupposed, 15–16, 86–7; differences among them, 15; synoptic and Johannine raise distinct problems, 16n; literary forms in, 18; and the primitive Christian community, 18–19; not the earliest writings, 40; and the doctrine of instrumentality, 49–50; as preaching, 51; subject to incompleteness of human observation, 52–3; subject to normal variations of narrative method, 53–6; importance of imagery and metaphor in, 56–7; other reasons for variations, 57–60; contradictions impossible, 61; not to be judged in terms of modern mentality, 62–3;

importance of author's intention, 63–4, 85–6; narrative modes should be studied, 65–6; theological value of less primitive textual elements, 69–70; not simply a subject to be studied, 70–1; source of spiritual life and preaching, 71–2, 87; novel interpretations to be used prudently in sermons, 72, 87–8; some contradictions only apparent, 73; importance of Church's interpretation of, 75, 85–6
Guitton, J., 18n
Gunkel, H., 17–18, 18n

H

Hermeneutics, general rule of, 32–3, 80–1
Historical method, necessity of, 15, 80–1
Humani generis, 59, 64n

I

Inerrancy of Gospels: because inspired by God, 14; not to be forgotten by exegete, 45, 86–7; its implications misunderstood, 45–7; not restricted to religious and moral content alone, 61–2, 69n
Inspiration: is an aspect of the problem raised by Form Criticism, 14, 45; and the Gospels, 15, 45, 86–7; and instrumentality, 48–9
Instruction of the Biblical Commission: aims, 9–10; need for, 13–14
Instrumentality, doctrine on: 48–9
Irenaeus, St, *Adversus haereses*, 87n

K

Kearns, C., 7n
Klineberg, O., 52n

L

Leo XIII: *see Vigilantiae, Providentissimus Deus*
Léon-Dufour, X., 17n, 18n
Literary criticism: source of Form Criticism, 17; determines "literary forms", 18; used to disprove historical elements of Gospels, 20–1; commended by *Divino afflante Spiritu*, 28n, 29–30; cannot assign theological value to categories of texts, 69–70; not to be pursued as an end in itself, 71
Literary forms: use by Form Criticism, 17–18, 20, 29, 30–3; relation to subject-matter, 28
Lohfink, N., 7n

M

McGinley, L. J., 17n
Martini, C., 22n
Musatti, C. L., 52n
Mussner, F., 18n, 24n

O

Our Father, the, 15, 68–9

P

Paul VI, 9n, 89
Pius XII; *see Divino afflante Spiritu, Humani generis*
Primitive Christian community: as *Sitz im Leben*, 18; more likely to produce legends than history, 19, 52n; creative, 19, 20, 22, 25–6; incapable of objectivity, 21; not anonymous but well known and well organized, 22
Providentissimus Deus, 16, 49n, 61 and n

Q

Quoniam in re biblica (Apostolic Letter), 71n, 74n, 87n, 88n

R

Radermakers, J., 8n
Riesenfeld, H., 17n
Rigaux, B., 18n
Ristow, H., and Mathiae, K., 18n, 67n
Robert, A., and Feuillet, A., 38n
Robinson, J. M., 17n

S

Schick, E., 17n
Schnackenburg, R., 18n
Schürmann, H., 67n
Sitz im Leben, 18
Spiritus Paraclitus, 29, 77n, 80n

T

Tacitus, 19 and n
Taylor, V., 17–18n
Tradition, stages of: task of exegete in regard to 33, 80–1, 82; the contribution of Jesus to, 34, 82–3; the contribution of the apostles to, 34ff, 36n, 83–4; the contribution of the evangelists to, 40–3, 84–5

V

Vatican Council, 9
Vigilantiae, 10, 76n, 80n

W

Woodworth, R., and Schlosberg, H., 52n